Letts **GCSE**

Success

Business Studies

Contents

Our economy

Inside and outside the business

People in business

Finance in business

Making the products

Selling the products

Our economy

Specialisation

Production Worker

Accountant

Sales Woman

In our economy, production of goods and services is normally indirect. People don't make goods or produce services for themselves, but instead work with others to provide these products. By doing this, they earn money. The products are then sold in the market-place, people buying them, with money acting as a medium of exchange.

- **Firms specialise in their own goods and services**, e.g. insurance firms, car manufacturers, banks, DIY stores
- This encourages owners to organise firms into specialist areas such as production, marketing and finance
- As a result, one part of the economy may depend on other parts, for example, specialist manufacturers rely on other specialist firms to insure, advertise and distribute their goods
- People also specialise, by training for specific jobs, e.g. accountants, welders, cashiers, teachers
- This **division of labour** allows a firm to employ specialists who use specialist machinery and equipment.

External influences

To sell their products, businesses must have a **demand** for these goods and services.
- The demand for many goods and services depends on the level of people's incomes.
- Changes occur in people's tastes and fashions.
- The sales of a firm's products will be affected by how successful its competitors' products are.

The success of a business will be influenced by government actions.
- The government creates various laws and regulations that affect business.
- The European Union (EU) and UK government also support firms, e.g. through providing financial assistance and advice.

Businesses are also influenced by what is happening in our society.
- Greater environmental awareness means that many people are interested in how a firm's activities affect the environment: their buying decisions are influenced by this.
- As a result, firms establish their own ethical policies.

The factors of production

These four factors of production are the **resources** that are used to produce the economy's goods and services.

Land

Businesses may:

- actually use the land, e.g. for agriculture, forestry or leisure activities
- build on the land (construction)
- extract raw materials from it, e.g. through mining and quarrying
- rent or buy land for their factories, offices and warehouses.

Capital

To make their goods or to provide their services, firms need to **invest** money in machinery, equipment, buildings, vehicles and other major resources. This investment is called 'capital'.

Labour

Businesses need to employ people to make and market their products. The UK's labour force is made up of all the men and women who are available to work.

Enterprise

The **entrepreneur** owns the business and is prepared to take the chance that his or her product will be a success. **Entrepreneurs are therefore also known as risk-takers**.

Each of these factors receives a financial reward:

- employees earn **wages**
- the owners of capital receive **interest**
- entrepreneurs make **profits**
- the owners of land receive **rent**.

KEY TERMS

Make sure you understand these terms before moving on!

- division of labour
- demand
- resources
- invest
- entrepreneur
- wages
- interest
- profits
- rent

QUICK TEST

1. The four factors of production are l_____, l_____, c_____ and e_____
2. What are the main external influences on UK firms?
3. Identify one advantage and one disadvantage from employees specialising.

Types of economy

All economies have limited resources and cannot provide all the goods and services that are demanded. As a result, they have to share out – allocate – these resources somehow. There are two main ways used by economies to allocate the resources.

Different economic systems

Free market economy
- Resources are owned by individuals
- Prices are set through demand and supply
- The **profit motive** encourages risk-takers (entrepreneurs)

Planned economy
- Resources are owned by the State
- Prices are set by the State
- Supply of goods and services does not depend on the profit motive

The free market system

Under this system, the working of the **price mechanism** solves what is produced. Ideally, demand and supply are in **equilibrium**: the demand for a product matches its supply level.

Where the demand for a product is greater than its supply:
- its price starts to rise
- this cuts the demand
- suppliers who have spare capacity will start making more
- the high price encourages other firms to start supplying the product
- supply will increase to meet the lower demand.

If the supply of a product is greater than its demand:
- its price starts to fall
- this increases its demand
- the lower price discourages some suppliers from selling the product
- supply will fall to meet the higher demand.

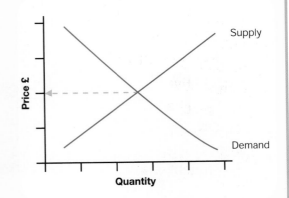

The price mechanism applies to the factors of production as well as to 'high-street' products.

The planned economy

service

Under this system, **the State** takes control of the economy's resources.
- It establishes price levels for the factors of production and the goods and services supplied.
- It decides what is produced, as well as how and where it is produced.
- In recent years, privatisation has led to many public-sector corporations being transferred to the private sector.
- This has sometimes led to a clash between the objective of providing a service and the objective of making a profit.

The mixed economy

All economies are part free market and part planned.
They are known as mixed economies. The UK's economy has a large private sector providing goods and services through the operation of the price mechanism. The public sector includes national services such as education and health, and local authority organisations.

Strengths of the private sector
- employers and employees can create their own personal wealth through the profit motive and hard work
- a greater range of products is supplied
- people have greater freedom to choose and buy what they want
- competition helps keep prices down and encourages new ideas.

Strengths of the public sector
- public services do not depend on the profit motive and will be supplied even at a loss
- the provision of basic services available to all (such as health services), regardless of people's ability to pay for them.

KEY TERMS

Make sure you understand these terms before moving on!
- profit motive
- price mechanism
- equilibrium
- privatisation
- private sector
- public sector

QUICK TEST

1. Which economic system does each point illustrate? Tick the relevant column.

	Free enterprise	Planned
a) Central planning is dominant	☐	☐
b) Prices are set through demand and supply	☐	☐
c) Competition is important	☐	☐
d) Prices are set by the central planning authority	☐	☐

Locating business

Business sectors and location

Businesses that need to locate are based in one of three sectors in our economy.

THE PRIMARY SECTOR
- **Primary sector businesses extract something:** e.g. coal, oil, stone, fish, iron ore.
- The location of these businesses usually depends on where the resources being extracted are found.

THE SECONDARY SECTOR
- **Businesses that construct or manufacture something** are in this sector.
- Their location is influenced by many factors, such as government support and the existence of a suitable labour force.

THE TERTIARY SECTOR
- **This 'service' sector supports the other two sectors.** Services include transport, finance, insurance, training and advertising.
- Their location will be influenced by the services required by firms in the other two sectors.

People and location

Entrepreneurs will want to ensure that their employees and customers are happy with where the business is located.

Geographical mobility of labour is where workers move to the work. However:
- people may not be willing to move to areas where there is work, e.g. due to family ties
- they may not be able to move because of higher living costs in the areas where there is work.

Occupational mobility of labour occurs where people train or retrain for new jobs
- however, some workers may find they cannot develop the new skills they need.

Customer convenience will influence location:
- in retailing, locating near to customers helps small shops survive
- if the business has a more convenient location than its competitors, it will gain at the expense of the competition.

Locating internationally

If a firm needs to locate internationally, its owners will take the following factors into account:
- avoiding any **trade barriers** that may exist
- coping with different cultures and languages
- avoiding countries with a history of political problems.

Influences on where businesses locate

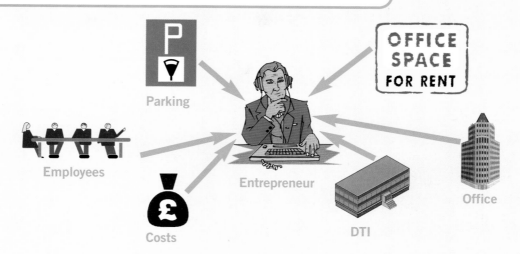

1. **What does it cost?** The cost of land varies from region to region.
2. **Is there a suitable labour force?** People must be able and willing to work where the business is located: if located in an expensive area, the business may have to pay higher wages and salaries.
3. **What is the business selling?** If it serves a local market, such as a hairdressing or plumbing business, it will locate near its customers; if it has a national market, it is less influenced by where its customers live.
4. **Is there government assistance?** The EU and the UK government support businesses locating in less well-off regions.
5. **What is the infrastructure?** The local infrastructure – transport and communications system – must be able to support the business efficiently.
6. **Is image relevant?** Some locations are valuable for certain types of business, and encourage firms to locate there (e.g. the City of London for a financial institution).

Be prepared to relate the general points about location to real-life business examples.

KEY TERMS

Make sure you understand these terms before moving on!
- geographical mobility
- occupational mobility
- trade barriers
- local market
- national market
- infrastructure

QUICK TEST

1. Classify each of these businesses as either primary, secondary or tertiary:
   a) a specialist distribution firm
   b) a builder
   c) a building society
   d) a forestry plantation
   e) a computer manufacturer
2. List four major influences on location.

The European Union

The 'EU 25'

Other countries such as Bulgaria and Romania are negotiating to join the EU.

Importance of the Union

The European Union contains four of the world's major economic powers: France, Germany, Italy and the United Kingdom. The EU is now the UK's main market.

UK Imports in 2004

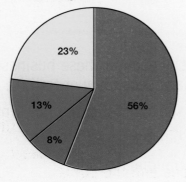

23%
13%
8%
56%

UK Exports in 2004

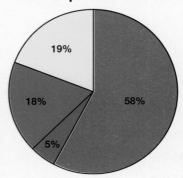

19%
18%
5%
58%

Many of the UK's laws are based on EU **directives** and **regulations**. The EU's influence includes:
- supporting equal treatment in the workplace
- protecting employees from exploitation
- encouraging greater industrial democracy by getting workers more involved in decision-making.

The EU's Social Charter protects the rights of workers, and covers areas of work such as working hours, the right to join a union, and health and safety.

The Single Market

Promoting trade between the member states was a major influence in establishing the EU. Its 'Common Market' is now a single market consisting of over 450 million people.

Examples of single market activity include:
- CE marking – if a product is to be sold or used within the EU it must carry the **CE mark** which indicates that the product has met with essential health and safety requirements set by the EU
- **competition policy** and merger control regulations – to control **monopolies** in member states so free and fair trade can take place
- **consumer protection** – including guaranteed information about prices and e-commerce providers, and protection against unfair advertising and unsafe products.

Influence of the Single Market

The Single Market has influenced UK business in several ways:
- common standards of quality and safety have been set, which UK firms must meet
- open markets encourage competition, requiring UK firms to be efficient to compete successfully
- free movement of labour and goods encourages employment and skill development.

 The Single Market brings both opportunities for, and competition to, UK business.

Monetary union

Most of the EU's member states are in the **Eurozone**, having agreed to adopt the **euro** as their future currency. The UK did not join the Eurozone in 1999. Economic and Monetary Union (**EMU**) is closely linked with the euro and Eurozone. The single currency will affect the EU:
- trade is much easier, because there is no need to change national currencies
- price differences will be much easier to see, as a result of the single currency.

KEY TERMS

Make sure you understand these terms before moving on!
- directive
- regulations
- Social Charter
- CE mark
- competition policy
- consumer protection
- Eurozone
- euro
- EMU

QUICK TEST

1. In the EU, what is the Social Charter?
2. What is the difference between the Eurozone and the euro?
3. What does the EU's Single Market seek to do?

International business

Why we trade internationally

- Our economy specialises in providing certain goods and services.
- We therefore create surpluses, which we trade with other countries.
- Some raw materials do not exist in the UK and so have to be imported.
- Certain goods cannot be produced in the UK, e.g. because of its climate.

 You should acknowledge that the UK is in the Single Market when answering questions on international trade.

Benefits from exporting

1. Sales increase
- businesses have a larger market in which to sell their products
- these markets are newer, and less saturated with their products than the UK market.

2. Economies of scale become possible
- as sales increase, the business gains from certain economies, e.g. being able to **bulk-buy** its raw materials at lower prices, or through using specialist machinery

- as a result, its lower unit costs make it more price-competitive.

3. Spreading the risk
- through trading in different markets, the business is not relying on a single market.
- it can expand its operations in other markets if one of its markets becomes difficult to trade in.

Benefits from importing

1. Lower costs
- the business may be able to obtain its supplies more cheaply from abroad
- these items may also be of better quality, and therefore better value for money, than those sold in the home market.

2. Greater choice
- businesses buying and selling directly to consumers (e.g. retailers) will improve their **product mix** from selling both home-produced and imported goods
- by doing so, they offer their customers greater choice.

Problems for businesses

Costs and prices
- When trading overseas, the business faces **exchange rate** fluctuations in the prices of the foreign currencies in which it must deal.
- This even applies in the Single Market, because the UK is not part of the Eurozone.
- These currency price changes make it **difficult for UK businesses to work out costs and set prices**.

Different culture and language
- Since overseas markets consist of people with other cultures, UK exporters will need to be aware of the differences in these cultures.
- Different languages also mean **the business must change how it markets its products**, e.g. re-labelling them in these other languages.
- **Communication** becomes more difficult with the overseas markets.

Competition from overseas
- UK-based firms face competition from businesses based in the overseas market, as well as from other **exporters** to that market.
- Overseas firms also compete in the UK economy.

Trade barriers
- The UK exporter may have to pay **tariffs** (import duties), a type of tax that raises the price of the item and makes it less competitive.
- **Quotas** – physical restrictions on the numbers of goods – may also affect a UK business when exporting to a particular overseas market.

Recording trade

The UK's balance of payments (2004)
Current account (£m)

Trade in goods	– 58 614
Trade in services	20 189
Total trade	– 38 425
Other adjustments	15 450
Current balance	– 22 975

- The balance of trade measures the UK's visible imports and exports.
- The Current account records trade in these goods, and also trade in services (invisibles).
- The Capital account shows the effect of buying and selling assets internationally.

KEY TERMS

Make sure you understand these terms before moving on!
- bulk-buy
- product mix
- exchange rate
- communication
- exporters
- tariff
- quota

QUICK TEST

1. What are the benefits for consumers from international trade?

2. For a UK-based firm, in what ways is trade in the Single Market a) similar to, and b) different from, trade outside the EU?

Sole trader and partnership businesses

Unincorporated

Both sole traders and partnerships are examples of unincorporated businesses. There are two major effects of being 'unincorporated'.

Unlimited liability
- The owners have **unlimited liability** for their business debts.
- If necessary, they may be forced to use their personal wealth to settle business debts.

Legal existence
- In law, the sole trader's business or the partners' business does not have a separate legal existence.
- This means that legal action is taken by or against the individual sole trader or partner, rather than in the name of the business.
- Business contracts are entered into by the owners rather than by the business.
- Because it does not have a separate legal existence, a change in ownership can end the business.

Sole traders

The sole trader remains the UK's most popular form of business. This business is **owned by a single individual**, although any number of people may be employed in the business by the owner.

Advantages of being a sole trader
- A small-scale business such as a sole trader only needs a relatively small amount of capital.
- The owner does not have to share profits with others.
- The owner is 'the boss'.
- It is quick and simple to set up in business as a sole trader, although the owner must register the business for tax purposes.
- Quick decisions can be made by the owner.

Disadvantages of being a sole trader
- Unlimited liability is the main drawback.
- Since there is no separate legal existence, the business does not automatically continue after the owner finishes.
- The small-scale nature of the business makes it difficult to obtain capital for expansion.
- 'The boss' has all the responsibility, and may have to work long hours.

Partnerships

These businesses can also be formed easily. The partners normally draw up a **partnership agreement** to record:

- how profits and losses will be shared
- the amount of capital invested by each partner
- individual rights (e.g. to a salary) and work responsibilities.

Compared with sole traders:

- partners can share decision-making, although this may lead to disputes between the partners
- responsibility can be shared, allowing individual partners more free time
- partners can specialise in different business functions
- more capital can usually be obtained by the partnership
- 'sleeping' partners may supply capital but will take no part in running the business.

 You may be asked to analyse the benefits of changing from a sole trader to a partnership.

Limited liability partnerships

The **limited liability** partnership (LLP) is a new form of partnership. The partnership is still easy to establish and its members gain from limited liability. They must draw up a members' agreement (similar to a partnership agreement).

Real-life businesses

- Sole traders and partners usually work in businesses with limited or local demand.
- Popular examples of sole traders include the 'corner shop', and small high-street businesses such as florists and hairdressers.
- Other service-based sole traders include craftspeople such as plumbers and electricians.

- Specialist firms such as antique shops often operate as sole traders or partnerships.
- Partnerships are commonly found in the 'professions', such as doctors, accountants and lawyers.

KEY TERMS

Make sure you understand these terms before moving on!

- unlimited liability
- capital
- tax
- partnership agreement
- limited liability

QUICK TEST

1. The two main features of being unincorporated are u_____ l_____ and no s_____ l_____ e_____.
2. What is the maximum number of people who can a) own, and b) work in, a sole trader business?
3. Find at least two examples of a) sole trader and b) partnership businesses in your local area.

Limited companies

An important benefit for a limited company is limited liability: the shareholders know exactly how much money they risk losing. This encourages people to invest, knowing there is a limit to the amount they can lose.

Being incorporated

Unlike sole traders and partnerships, a limited company is an incorporated business. As a result:

- **the company has a separate legal existence** from that of its owners (shareholders) – so legal action will be taken in the name of the limited company

- shareholders (and other people) can sue the company

- this separate legal existence means the company has greater continuity, because its existence is not ended by the death or retirement of its shareholders

- the owners have **limited liability** for their business debts so they **cannot be made to use their own wealth to settle any business debts**.

Ownership versus control

Limited companies face a separation of ownership from control.

- The company's shareholders tend to have little say in the daily running of the company.

- It is the company's directors who control the company.

- These directors are elected by the shareholders at the company's annual general meeting (AGM).

- **The shareholders and directors may have different views and objectives**, for example different opinions on the speed of the company's growth and the levels of its profit.

Company documents

- **The memorandum of association** outlines the company's external relationship; it states the company's name and its purpose, and where its registered office is located.

- **The articles of association document** records the company's internal workings, e.g. of directors and their election.

- The company will also publish its final accounts: the PLC's accounts can be obtained by members of the public.

Private and public

Private limited companies must include the word limited in their name, and public companies the words public limited company. The abbreviations **ltd** and **plc** are widely used.

Advantages of being private

- Private companies can keep their business affairs more private because members of the public (and therefore competitors) do not have access to their accounts.

- Private companies are less likely than PLCs to suffer from bureaucracy ('red tape') and from diseconomies of scale (their unit costs start to rise).

- Compared with PLCs, ownership of a private company is not so subject to hostile takeover bids because its shares cannot be bought on the Stock Exchange.

> *You are often assessed on your understanding of the difference between private companies and PLCs.*

Advantages of being public

- PLCs can raise capital from members of the public, unlike private companies.

- PLCs are usually larger than private companies, and therefore gain from economies of scale.

- PLCs are more likely to be able to employ specialists, and to use specialist machinery and equipment.

- Through their greater size and their ability to ask the public to buy shares, PLCs find it easier to obtain capital.

> *Be careful to distinguish between a public company and the public sector.*

KEY TERMS

Make sure you understand these terms before moving on!
- limited company
- incorporated business
- shareholder
- director
- annual general meeting
- ltd
- plc
- economy of sale

QUICK TEST

1. State two differences between private and public limited companies.

2. Why is the separation of ownership from control important?

3. Identify two differences between incorporated and unincorporated businesses.

Other businesses

Multinationals

A multinational has its headquarters in one country, and carries out operations in other countries. In the UK, multinationals are normally PLCs.

Multinationals have developed because:

- they can gain from low-cost labour and other **factors of production** – e.g. producing in low-wage countries cuts production costs and makes the multinational's products more price-competitive
- they can sometimes avoid **trade barriers** – e.g. many multinationals have set up business in the UK and other EU countries in order to avoid paying the Single Market's common external tariff
- they are able to spread risk by **diversifying** into different countries' markets.

For and against multinationals

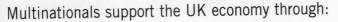

Multinationals support the UK economy through:

- providing jobs, which helps to reduce unemployment
- bringing in new expertise and new technology
- bringing in new ideas (e.g. successful work practices from the Far East).

The drawbacks of multinationals operating in our economy are:

- they are in a strong bargaining position and can influence the government's policies
- different work practices can lead to disputes
- they may export their profits.

Co-operatives

- **Producer (or worker) co-operatives** are created when people join together to provide a product. In the UK, some worker co-operatives were created by employees buying out their company because it was in financial difficulties.
- **Retail co-operatives** are created when consumers join together to buy in bulk.
- Individual retail co-operatives are supplied by the CWS, the Co-operative Wholesale Society.

Franchises

A franchise is created when a person goes into business to sell a named product from a major supplier. The person taking out the franchise – the franchisee – supplies the capital, and in return receives training, the product, marketing expertise and general support from the franchisor. Examples of franchising companies include McDonald's and other major 'fast-food' chains, and The Body Shop.

Advantages of franchising

- Advantages to the franchisee – gaining a well-known product, trading name and reputation, and receiving the franchisor's expert support.
- Advantages to the franchisor – gaining outlets without having to find the capital to finance them, and a willing franchisee who is likely to work hard to make a success of the franchise.

Public corporations

Public corporations are what are sometimes called nationalised industries. **These organisations are owned by the State**, and supply goods and services to the whole economy.

- The Conservative governments of the 1980s privatised many public corporations on the grounds that these industries were inefficient, suffered from diseconomies of scale, and would therefore be more efficient under private ownership.

Arguments in favour of public ownership are:
- it is a way of controlling natural monopolies
- it guarantees that essential services will be provided
- certain areas of the economy (e.g. defence) need to be controlled centrally because of national security.

Local authority businesses

Many local authorities operate businesses such as sports centres, or use land to obtain revenue (e.g. from car parking charges). These may be profit-making activities, which provide revenue for the local authority.

KEY TERMS

Make sure you understand these terms before moving on!
- factors of production
- diversify
- franchisee
- franchisor
- public corporation
- local authority

QUICK TEST

1. List two benefits and two drawbacks to a country from having multinationals in its economy.

2. The organisation creating the franchise is the f_____ , and people who buy franchises from it are the f_____.

3. What are the two main forms of co-operative?

Stakeholders in business

Business objectives

Private sector businesses are owned by individuals, who may have a number of different **objectives**. These objectives are set by the entrepreneurs, and often include:

- **survival** – the owners will want the business to survive, and may therefore put up with losses in the short term
- profit – a **profit target** will be set, so that the owners receive this as a reward for risking their money
- **growth** – by growing in size, larger organisations find it easier to survive, e.g. by diversifying (selling different products in different markets) and through gaining economies of scale
- **market share** – the larger the share of the market, the more dominant the firm can be, e.g. by setting price levels.

Public sector organisations are owned by the State, whose officials (e.g. politicians) set the objectives for these businesses. The objectives may be more to do with providing an efficient service than with making profits.

Internal stakeholders

Entrepreneurs

Entrepreneurs are particularly interested in their firm's survival, and the likelihood of profits. This profit motive may clash with the objectives of other stakeholder groups. For example:

- customers want low prices, which cut profit margins
- employees want high pay and job security, which may conflict with the push for profits
- lenders and suppliers are more interested in the organisation's **liquidity** – its ability to pay the debts owed to them.

Employees

All employees will wish to see the business be successful, to keep their jobs and income. They may also benefit through **share ownership** or **profit-sharing** schemes.

- Owners and managers are usually keen to consult with the employees about their work and feelings.

External stakeholders

Shareholders

As the owners of limited companies, shareholders have an interest in the company's financial performance. **In some companies the main shareholders are also directors or managers**, and therefore internal to the company.

- Although ordinary shareholders own the profits of the company, it is the directors who decide how much profit will be distributed to the ordinary shareholders.

Customers

Customers have opinions on how the business operates.

- They sometimes join together to act as a consumer pressure group.
- If they are unhappy with the firm's work, or with the quality of its products, they will stop being customers.

Lenders

Lenders are stakeholders, for the following reasons.

- They have invested money in the business.
- They expect to receive a return on their investment (e.g. interest payments).
- They want their money back in future.

The community

The local population are also stakeholders. They are particularly interested in the organisation's:

- employment policy – it is a source of work for them
- environmental policy – this affects their quality of life.

The organisation may create **positive externalities**, such as better local roads and transport, but it can also create **negative externalities** such as pollution.

KEY TERMS

Make sure you understand these terms before moving on!

- objective
- survival
- profit target
- growth
- market share
- liquidity
- share ownership
- profit-sharing

QUICK TEST

1. What is a 'stakeholder'?
2. For each stakeholder group, suggest one area of interest in the firm's work:
   a) Shareholders
   b) Directors
   c) Employees
   d) Customers
   e) Local community
   f) Lenders

Practice questions

Use the questions to test your progress.
Check your answers on page 94.

1. List **three** examples of industries in the secondary sector.

   ....

2. Which of the following is a factor of production?
   a) Supply   ☐
   b) Franchise   ☐
   c) Profit   ☐
   d) Labour   ☐

3. Tick the phrase that best explains the term 'limited liability':

   The business is limited to the products it is allowed to make   ☐
   The owners are limited to the amount they can lose in the business   ☐
   The number of meetings that can be held is limited   ☐
   The business has a maximum number of 20 owners   ☐
   The amount of capital that can be invested is limited   ☐
   Employees are limited as to what they can do in the business   ☐

4. The following features are associated with either a sole trader, a partnership, or one of the types of limited company. For each, identify the most appropriate form of business ownership:
   a) The owners usually create a written agreement

   ....

   ....

   b) All profits go to the owner, who also bears all the losses

   ....

   c) There are typically from 2 to 20 owners

   ....

   d) Economies of scale are most likely

   ....

   e) Shares can be issued, but not advertised for sale to the public at large

   ....

5. Explain briefly how the price mechanism operates.

   ....

   ....

6. Oakworth Ltd makes garden sheds and other wooden products. It originally started as a partnership, but the owners converted it to a private limited company. As the business has continued to grow, one owner has suggested turning it into a PLC.
   a) Give **two** reasons why the owners might have decided to change the business to a limited company.

   ....

   ....

   b) Why might the other owner of Oakworth Ltd want to keep it as a private company?

   ....

   ....

7. In December 2005 Jim Bentley was made redundant. He wanted to use the redundancy money to buy a small shop. Jim has been offered a franchise with a major petrol supplier. He now runs a garage and forecourt shop.

a) What names are given to:

i) a person like Jim who invests in a franchise?

....

ii) the companies that sell franchises?

....

b) Suggest **two** advantages and **two** disadvantages to Jim in entering into a franchise rather than becoming a traditional sole trader

....

....

c) Identify **two** business objectives Jim is likely to have ....

....

d) How might these objectives differ from those of the petrol company? ....

....

8. Putitin Ltd makes metal containers that it sells to other businesses. The company is located in the Midlands. The directors are investigating whether the company can start exporting to the rest of the EU. If they decide to export, they will consider relocating the business to south-east England.

a) In which sector of production, and in which sector of the economy, is Putitin Ltd based?

....

....

b) i) Identify **two** stakeholder groups this company will have.

....

....

ii) For each group, explain why it is interested in the company's performance.

....

....

c) What benefits and problems might Putitin Ltd face if it starts trading with the rest of the EU?

....

....

d) Explain how exporting to the rest of the EU will differ from exporting to non-EU countries in Europe.

....

....

e) Explain **four** factors that the directors will consider when taking the decision to relocate.

....

....

....

....

The main functions of business

Production of goods and services

Modern production

Lean production can overcome some of mass production's drawbacks, e.g. by using capacity and improving morale.
'Just-in-time' reduces the costs of stockholding, but any delivery problem can halt all production.

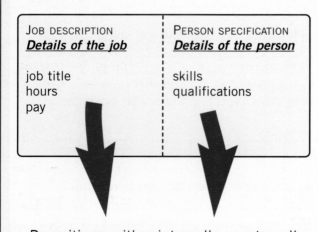

Method of production

Job production occurs where a single product is made to customer requirements.

Batch production involves making similar items in set numbers ('batches').

Mass production creates large numbers of identical, standardised products. This type of production often leads to economies of scale.

Human resource management (HRM)

Employing

JOB DESCRIPTION ***Details of the job***	PERSON SPECIFICATION ***Details of the person***
job title hours pay	skills qualifications

- Recruiting – either internally or externally
- Selecting – interviews, aptitude and other tests
- Appointing – issuing the contract of employment
- Inducting – introducing the new employee to the firm

Training

After induction training, the firm will offer more training, either internal or external.

- On-the-job **internal training** is specific to the firm, but may be delivered by non-specialists.
- Off-the-job **external training** is delivered by trained staff, but is not exclusively for the firm.

Other work of HRM

Other functions of the HRM (personnel) department include:

- negotiating with trade unions and other employee associations
- paying wages and salaries.

Finance – the accounting function

Looking forward
Budgets plan for the future and set performance targets.
- Cash budgeting helps to ensure liquidity.
- Fixed and variable costs are analysed to calculate the firm's break-even point.

Looking back
Financial accounting:
- records financial transactions
- calculates the firm's profit or loss
- displays the firm's assets and liabilities
- assesses the firm's performance (through accounting ratios).

Obtaining finance
The finance may come from:
- internal sources – personal savings or retained profits
- external sources – long-term capital such as shares and debentures, and short-term capital, e.g. trade credit, bank overdraft.

Marketing – promoting and selling

A product's market can often be broken down into different **market segments** – e.g. by age and income. **Market research** is necessary to provide information about the firm's 'marketing mix'. This 'mix' consists of:

Product: Product differentiation is important. Firms also analyse product life cycles.

Price: High price strategies include skimming, maximising and premium pricing. Low-price ones include penetration and capturing.

Place: The product will need to be distributed through channels – e.g. by wholesalers to retailers.

Promotion: The four main methods are advertising, sales promotion, direct marketing and personal selling. The Internet has increased in importance as an advertising/promotion medium.

KEY TERMS

Make sure you understand these terms before moving on!
- lean production
- 'just-in-time'
- internal training
- external training
- budget
- financial accounting
- market segment
- market research

QUICK TEST

1. Why do firms carry out cash budgeting?
2. What is the difference between a job description and a person specification?
3. State the four main methods of promotion.

Organising business

There will be a close link between a firm's objectives and the way it is organised (its structure).

■ Most private sector firms are organised by function.

■ Central and local government organisations are normally organised by the service they offer.

Organisational terms

An organisation will have a **hierarchy**, shown by its organisation chart. The status of employees in the hierarchy is shown by the **chain of command**, which runs from the directors to the managers, then through the departments to the shop floor and office workers.

Managers need to **delegate** some decisions and tasks to their staff (their subordinates). This delegation flows down the chain of command.

When delegating, **the manager must give the member of staff the authority** to make the decision and to do the task. By doing so, **the employee now has the responsibility** to do the work, and **becomes accountable to the manager**.

Where a lot of delegation exists, the firm is likely to have a decentralised structure: little delegation is associated with a more centralised structure.

The number of staff under an individual manager's control indicates that manager's **span of control**.

Tall and flat structures

A firm's structure may be tall or flat. This indicates the number of levels found in the firm's hierarchy.

A **tall structure** is associated with:

■ long chains of command
■ narrow spans of control
■ specialised staff
■ slower decision-making
■ formal communication systems.

As a result, many firms use a **flat structure**, to speed up communication and cut out bureaucracy (red tape). This is known as delayering.

Organisation by function

This form of organisation illustrates a role culture, with clearly defined job descriptions, chains of command and lines of communication.

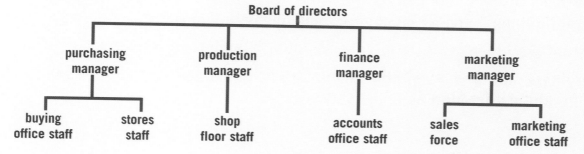

- The role of the organisation chart is to show the firm's internal structure.
- It shows chains of command as a series of lines, illustrating the line authority of departmental managers.
- The chart can become out-of-date.
- It will not show the informal communication that will exist.
- It is not always easy to show on the chart those employees who have a specialist staff function.

Organisation by task

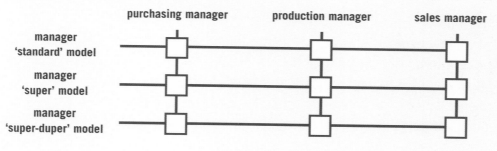

- One effect of 'flattening' an organisation's structure is that emphasis may move from the traditional department towards a more task-based structure.
- This is called a matrix structure.
- Staff from different departments work together on set tasks and projects.
- Matrix organisation often exists in flatter structures, where managers have wide spans of control.

KEY TERMS

Make sure you understand these terms before moving on!
- hierarchy
- chain of command
- delegate
- span of control
- tall structure
- flat structure
- matrix

QUICK TEST

1. What is the difference between 'span of control' and 'chain of command'?
2. Why have many firms attempted to 'flatten' their organisational structure?
3. Draw the organisation chart for a business you have studied.

Communicating in business

There are many groups with whom the organisation must communicate. These include:

■ internal groups, such as managers, employees, union representatives

■ external groups, e.g. shareholders, suppliers, lenders, customers.

In every case, the *communication* should be as quick as is required, as clear as possible, and as detailed as necessary.

Forms of communication

Oral communication
■ Meetings are (usually) formal settings for oral communication.
■ The telephone is often the main method of communicating orally with suppliers.
■ Oral communication tends to be quicker than written forms, and allows interpretation and further discussion.
■ It lacks the permanent nature of written communication: it cannot easily be stored and referred to later.

Written communication
■ Letters are sent mainly externally as formal communication, whereas memos tend to be used internally for more informal communication.
■ Email is a popular way of sending memos and letters electronically.
■ Company magazines and notices are sometimes transmitted as email attachments.
■ The annual report and accounts will be sent in written form to shareholders.
■ Reports are written on major areas of development or concern, e.g. progress of a new product.
■ A written record of meetings is kept as minutes, and the agenda will also be in written form.

Visual communication
■ This form of communication is used to simplify and summarise words and numbers.
■ Organisations use pictures, charts, graphs and other forms of visual display.

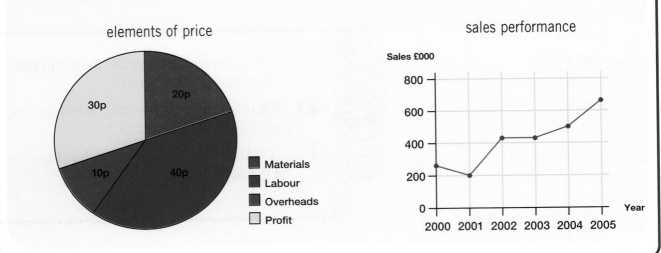

elements of price

sales performance

Communication theory

The key elements in using communication are: the **transmitter** (sender of the message); the **recipient** (receiver of the message); the **message** itself; and the communication **medium** by which the message is being sent. In business, all these elements must function effectively.

Good communication

Good communication is influenced by:
- the attitudes of the sender and receiver
- their knowledge of the subject – matter being communicated
- what is being communicated – sending instructions, giving advice, asking for opinions or presenting facts
- how it is being communicated – the suitability of the communication medium used
- the amount of noise present (anything that affects the message being transmitted and received).

Communication in trading

There will be a flow of **trading documents** between buyer and seller.

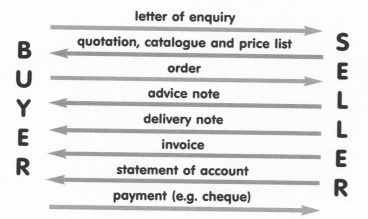

The **invoice** is the main trading document. It contains:
- details of the goods ordered
- information on delivery
- any VAT and settlement discount being offered.

 Remember: communication may have to be stored, retrieved and transmitted.

KEY TERMS

Make sure you understand these terms before moving on!
- communication
- transmitter
- recipient
- message
- medium
- trading document
- invoice

QUICK TEST

1. With which major groups will an organisation need to communicate?
2. What influences how the organisation communicates its information?
3. What are the main causes of poor communication?

How a business grows

Integration

In a **merger** two companies agree to join.

This external growth is the quickest way for organisations to grow.

In a **takeover** one company buys enough of another company's voting shares to take control.

 This topic links closely with economies of scale.

Types of integration

HORIZONTAL: between companies in the same industry and at the same stage of production. **This integration increases market share and power, and leads to economies of scale**.

VERTICAL: between companies in the same industry but at different stages of production. **This form of integration strengthens control over supply and sales of the products**.
- Vertical backwards is when the company controls firms back down the chain of production.
- Vertical forwards is when the company controls firms closer to the final customer.

LATERAL (conglomerate): between companies in different industries. **This integration helps the company diversify into different markets, which reduces risk**. If one market fails, the company can continue trading in its other market(s).

Measuring size

Several methods are used to measure an organisation's size: there is no one best method for all organisations.

OFFICE SUPPLY

profits
how much the business keeps from selling its goods/services

turnover
the sales that the business makes

employees
the number of people employed in the business

capital employed
the resources the business has invested in it

Internal growth

Organisations can grow organically (internally) as well as through mergers or takeovers. This internal form of growth happens when an organisation:

- sells more of its existing products
- starts selling new products
- enters new markets.

KEY TERMS

Make sure you understand these terms before moving on!
- merger
- takeover
- horizontal
- vertical
- lateral

QUICK TEST

1. Distinguish between:
   a) internal and external growth
   b) mergers and takeovers
   c) horizontal, vertical and lateral growth.
2. State two benefits arising from growth.
3. Name four methods that can be used to measure the size of a business
4. What are the three ways for an organisation to grow organically?

Supporting business

The range of government support given

Financial support
- Financial support comes mainly from central government and from the European Union.
- Examples include financial support for the less well off regions of the UK, and support through training and employment.

Government policies
- Governments consider the effect on business when changing their taxation and interest rate policies.
- Government legislation helps protect firms against unfair competition.

Information
- Local and national government provide support through information.
- The government's Office for National Statistics (**ONS**) publishes important statistical summaries that organisations use. These include: Regional Trends; Social Trends; and Economic Trends.

Exporting
- Support for exporters comes from British Trade International, which gives information, advice and assistance.
- The Export Credit Guarantee Department provides guarantees and insurance against losses through exporting.

The DTI

The Department for Trade and Industry (**DTI**) supports UK firms in different ways. Examples include:

- help for small businesses

- providing information and advice on EU developments

- offering free booklets and 'best practice' guides

- supporting firms wishing to use new technologies.

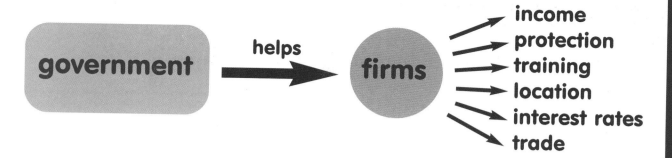

government **helps** → firms →

- income
- protection
- training
- location
- interest rates
- trade

The European Union

- The EU offers financial support through funds such as its Regional Development Fund, which helps support poorer regions.
- The EU also provides support through information.
- The **Single Market** is probably the greatest assistance given to efficient UK firms, through removing trade barriers and allowing free access to EU markets.

Other support

Other organisations, such as local **Chambers of Commerce** and the **Confederation of British Industry**, also support businesses.

KEY TERMS

Make sure you understand these terms before moving on!

- ONS
- DTI
- Single Market
- Chamber of Commerce
- Confederation of British Industry

QUICK TEST

1. List three areas of assistance given to UK businesses by the UK government.
2. Give two reasons why the UK government wishes to support UK firms.
3. Name two publications issued by the ONS.

Business and the law

Controls and protection

All organisations face controls through laws, rules and regulations. Other laws exist to protect people and other firms.

Activities that are controlled include:
- where the organisation operates → controlling its location and its development
- what it has to pay → controlling its tax

Areas of protection include
- people with whom it deals → protecting its employees and its customers
- those who share its marketplace → protecting its competitors

Protecting employees

Individual employees are in a weak position compared with their employers. As a result, UK and EU laws safeguard employees, particularly in the areas of employment, discrimination, and health and safety.

Employment
Employees working under a contract of employment are protected against **unfair dismissal**.
The EU is a major influence on employment law.
- limiting working time to a normal maximum of 48 hours per week
- giving employees the right to unpaid leave following the birth of a child
- ensuring equal treatment for part-time staff.

Discrimination
Acts that protect workers against discrimination include:
- the **Race Relations Acts**, which make it illegal to discriminate on the grounds of race, nationality or ethnic origin
- the **Disability Discrimination Act**, which makes it unlawful to discriminate against a person on the grounds of disability
- the **Equal Pay Act** and the **Sex Discrimination Acts**, which seek to protect against unequal pay and treatment between the sexes.

Health
The **Health and Safety at Work Act** outlines duties concerning matters of health and safety. The employer must provide safe:
- working conditions
- machinery
- working processes
- entry and exit.

In return, employees must take care of themselves and others at work, not interfere with safety items, notify the employer of safety problems, and co-operate with the employer on safety matters.

Protecting consumers

Since individual consumers are usually in a weak bargaining position with the large organisations they buy from, there are many UK and EU laws to protect them.

- The **Sale and Supply of Goods Act** requires goods that are sold to:
  - be of satisfactory quality
  - be fit for the purpose for which they are intended
  - match their description.
- The **Trade Descriptions Acts** make it a criminal offence to give a false description of goods.
- **EU Directives** also protect consumers. For example, there are directives on:
  - Electronic Commerce (information providers must provide certain information to users of e-commerce)
  - Price Indication (selling prices and other details must be displayed)
  - Misleading Advertising (protection against unfair adverts)
  - CE Marking (products meeting safety and other standards can carry the CE mark).

Protecting competition

Monopolies – where one firm dominates a market – are discouraged, because **the monopoly firm can set its own prices (no competition) and exploit consumers**. The UK government encourages competition through the **price mechanism**, with its interaction of supply and demand.

- The Office of Fair Trading (OFT) can examine the trading activities of a firm.
- The Competition Act protects firms against the anti-competitive practices of other firms.
- The Competition Commission works with the OFT to ensure that proposed mergers between large companies are in the interests of consumers.
- The EU's competition policy seeks to protect consumers against unfair monopolies.

KEY TERMS

Make sure you understand these terms before moving on!
- Race Relations Act
- Disability Discrimination Act
- Equal Pay Act
- Sex Discrimination Act
- Health and Safety at Work Act
- Sale of Supply of Goods Act
- Trade Descriptions Act
- monopoly

QUICK TEST

1. Employees are protected against exploitation by their employers in the areas of e_____, d_____ and h_____.

2. Why are monopolies discouraged in the UK economy?

Other influences on business

Pressure groups

- A 'pressure group' is a **group of people who share similar interests, and who wish to further their interests by influencing others**.

- A pressure group may be local, such as a local residents' association campaigning against pollution from a local factory.

- The group may be national, such as the Automobile Association, which campaigns on behalf of UK motorists, or international (e.g. Greenpeace or Friends of the Earth).

- **Trade unions** have been influential pressure groups for many years, acting on behalf of their members.

- The TUC (Trades Union Congress) and the CBI (Confederation of British Industry) are national pressure groups campaigning for unions and employers respectively, hoping to influence government and EU policy.

- In recent years, other pressure groups have had a large influence on the work of business. In particular, **environmental pressure groups have often persuaded firms to change policies and production methods**.

- Many companies have responded by creating their own **ethical policies**. These policies often outline ways in which the company could avoid exploitation of 'third world' people and resources.

Consumer organisations

- The UK government has set up many 'watchdogs' that regulate our major industries.

- These regulators protect consumers and others from exploitation by organisations in industries such as water, power and telecommunications.

Examples of organisations that support the consumer include:

- the Citizens Advice Bureau, an organisation with offices in most towns where voluntary staff help consumers with a range of problems

- the Advertising Standards Authority (ASA), which is financed by the advertising industry and which oversees advertising (other than on TV or radio).

STEP – Social, Technological, Economic and Political – influences

Social

- Social influences are important because businesses now recognise the importance of a good image.
- This image is helped when the business recognises the **social responsibility** it has, for example to its customers, employees and shareholders.
- These influences also include changes in society (e.g. tastes and fashion).
- Changing social trends also include the increase in the average age of the population, which affects the demand for different goods and services.

Technological

- Technological developments have made some industries grow rapidly, such as the telecommunications industry with its mobile-phone market, and have forced other industries to adapt (e.g. banking, to electronic funds transfer).

Economic

- Economic influences include the level of **consumer demand** for a firm's goods or services.
- Government economic policy, such as its influence on **interest rates** (the cost of borrowing) is also important.

Political

- The government's political policies, creating new laws that affect business, are a major influence on firms.

Social **T**echnological **E**conomic **P**olitical

KEY TERMS

Make sure you understand these terms before moving on!

- pressure group
- trade union
- ethical policy
- social responsibility
- consumer demand
- interest rate

QUICK TEST

1 a) One example of a social influence is:
_____ .

b) One example of a technological influence is:
_____ .

c) One example of an economic influence is:
_____ .

d) One example of a political influence is:
_____ .

2 In what ways do trade unions seek to influence firms?

3 What is a pressure group?

Practice questions

Use the questions to test your progress.
Check your answers on page 94.

1. The formal structure of a large organisation is shown by its:
   a) market share ☐
   b) balance sheet ☐
   c) mission statement ☐
   d) organisation chart ☐

2. Safety standards for manufacturers are set by government and EU:
   a) accounts ☐
   b) taxes ☐
   c) laws ☐
   d) statistics ☐

3. Email has become a popular method of communicating information. Identify which of these are advantages of sending emails, and which are disadvantages:
   a) transmission is instantaneous
   b) large amounts of information can be sent
   c) users must have a computer
   d) multiple copies of the email can be sent
   e) no hard copy is immediately available.

4. Classify each of the following forms of integration:
   a) two insurance companies merging
   b) an oil company takes over a chain of petrol stations
   c) a tobacco company takes over a food processing company
   d) a high-street clothing retailer takes over a clothing manufacturer
   e) a newspaper group buys a competitor publisher's business.

Horizontal	Vertical forwards	Vertical backwards	Lateral

5. For each of the following situations, identify the most appropriate law:

   a) Sex Discrimination
   b) Race Relations
   c) Data Protection
   d) Disability Discrimination
   e) Health and Safety at Work
   f) Equal Pay

   i) Brian's job advert states 'white people only'
   ii) Jenny and Mike do exactly the same job, but Mike receives a higher salary
   iii) Jason blocks open a fire door
   iv) Sarah is not considered for promotion because she is female
   v) John asks to see his personnel records
   vi) Natalie refuses to attend training on fire prevention
   vii) A wheelchair user wants to talk to the directors about difficult access to work

6. Give **three** reasons why a company benefits from owning businesses at every stage of production.

   ....
   ....
   ....
   ....

7. This is the organisation chart for Tastystuff Ltd, a food manufacturer. Study the chart and answer the questions.

```
                              ┌─────────────┐
                              │  Managing   │
                              │  Director   │
                              └──────┬──────┘
        ┌────────────────┬──────────┴──────────┬────────────────────┐
┌───────┴────────┐ ┌─────┴──────┐ ┌────────────┴───────┐ ┌──────────┴─────┐
│   Production   │ │ Marketing  │ │  Human Resources   │ │   Financial    │
│   Director     │ │ Director   │ │     Director       │ │   Director     │
└───────┬────────┘ └─────┬──────┘ └────────┬───────────┘ └──────┬─────────┘
   ┌────┴─────┐          │          ┌───────┴──────┐             │
┌──┴───┐ ┌────┴─────┐ ┌──┴────┐ ┌───┴─────┐ ┌──────┴────┐ ┌──────┴───────┐
│Works │ │Production│ │Sales  │ │Staff    │ │Recruitment│ │Accounts      │
│Manager│ │Controller│ │Manager│ │Welfare  │ │Manager    │ │Office Manager│
└──┬───┘ └────┬─────┘ └──┬────┘ │Manager  │ └─────┬─────┘ └──────┬───────┘
   │          │          │      └─────────┘       │              │
┌──┴───┐ ┌────┴─────┐ ┌──┴────┐           ┌───────┴──────┐ ┌─────┴────┐
│Works │ │Production│ │Marketing│         │Human Resources│ │Accounts  │
│Office│ │Office    │ │Office  │          │Office Staff   │ │Office    │
│Staff │ │Staff     │ │Staff   │          └──────────────┘ │Staff     │
└──────┘ └──────────┘ └────────┘                           └──────────┘
```

a) Name **three** other departments or sections Tastystuff Ltd may have, but which are not shown on this chart.

....
....
....

b) Explain the work of the Human Resources function in Tastystuff Ltd.

....
....

c) Use this chart to explain the terms 'hierarchy', 'span of control' and 'chain of command'.

....
....
....

d) Explain **three** reasons why organisation charts are drawn up.

....
....
....

e) i) Identify **one** reason why the Accounts Office staff will need to communicate with the Human Resources Office staff.

....

ii) Suggest **two** methods of internal communication that might be used between the staff in this situation. Justify your choice.

....
....

iii) Explain why good communication is important to Tastystuff Ltd.

....
....

Employing staff

Why recruit?

Many businesses draw up a **workforce plan** to help them meet future staffing needs.
A workforce plan **helps the business cope with changing employment patterns**, such as:
- the increase in part-time employment
- more women seeking work
- an ageing population.

Recruiting staff

Internal recruitment
- Morale improves because staff realise there are promotion opportunities, although the morale of colleagues who did not get the job may fall.
- The person appointed already knows work routines and procedures.
- Recruitment costs are lower, but no new ideas from outside will be introduced into the business.

External recruitment
- Although more costly, there will be a wider range of applicants from which to choose.
- Recruiting externally brings in new blood and new ideas.

How to recruit

With internal recruitment, the post must be brought to the attention of all employees. This is done by using notice-boards, staff magazines or circulars (e.g. by email). When advertising externally for staff, the business can choose from various sources.
- Newspapers and magazines – national papers and specialist magazines for professional posts, and local papers for less high-level and specialist staff.
- Jobcentres – these provide employment advice as well as having details of local jobs.
- Employment agencies – these businesses will try to find suitable employees, for a fee.
- Direct contact – businesses may contact schools, colleges or training agencies for staff.

Job analysis

This is used to find out the various tasks and responsibilities of a particular job. It consists of two main elements.
- The **job description** contains the job title, details of where it is based, with whom the job holder will work, and a summary of the main activities.
- The **person specification** lists the qualifications, experience and skills a person will need to carry out the job.

Selecting staff

HRM staff study the work records of internal applicants. They will send external applicants an application form, or ask them to submit their CVs (**Curriculum Vitae**). A **shortlist** will be drawn up by comparing applicants with the post's job description and person specification.

Applicants are normally interviewed.
- Although this is expensive for the business, the interviewer can assess the interviewee's appearance, confidence and knowledge, and ask relevant questions.
- Interview is a two-way process, since the interviewee also has the chance to ask questions.

Selection tests

These are set at interview. They include:
- aptitude tests to see if the candidate can do the work required
- intelligence tests designed to check the candidate's mental abilities
- personality tests to discover the applicant's personality type.

Appointing staff

The HRM staff will take up and check the successful applicant's references, and later issue a **contract of employment**. The contract contains:
- names of employer and employee, and the start date of the employment
- details of hours, pay, pension, sick pay, holidays and holiday pay
- the length of notice required
- disciplinary rules.

KEY TERMS

Make sure you understand these terms before moving on!
- workforce plan
- internal recruitment
- external recruitment
- job description
- person specification
- curriculum vitae
- shortlist
- contract of employment

QUICK TEST

1. Of which form of recruitment – internal or external – are the following characteristics?

   Tick the appropriate column.

	Internal recruitment	External recruitment
a) All existing staff need to be notified	☐	☐
b) Adverts for staff may be placed in newspapers	☐	☐
c) An employment agency may be used	☐	☐
d) Recruitment costs are relatively low	☐	☐

2. Delete which does not apply:
   a) Details of the qualifications required to do the job are listed in the person specification/job description

   b) The main activities to be undertaken by the post holder are listed in the person specification/job description

Training and developing staff

The nature, amount and quality of training carried out will depend on the cost and on the resources available.

■ Some organisations have their own training departments, whereas others rely on specialist training organisations or on government initiatives.

■ The government is a major influence, e.g. by creating training schemes such as the Modern Apprenticeship scheme.

Why train staff?

■ Staff **training** and development take place so that new and existing employees work as efficiently as possible to help the business meet its objectives.

■ Staff also have to cope with changes to their work, e.g. as a result of technological developments, and training will be required.

■ Training also prepares staff for future promotion: they 'grow' as the business grows.

The business gains through creating a good reputation as well as ensuring it has staff with the right skills.

 Any programme of training must consider the needs of the business and the needs of the employee.

Induction training

Induction training introduces the firm to the new employee, and the new employee to the firm. The new employees need to learn about:

■ the firm's objectives, its working practices and its rules

■ their role and responsibilities in the firm

■ the environment in which they will be working.

The length of the induction depends on the importance and degree of difficulty of the job.

On-the-job training

This internal approach is the simplest form of staff training and development. The employee is trained by someone who already has the appropriate knowledge, skills and experience.

On-the-job training:

■ is often less costly than off-the-job training

■ concentrates exclusively on the needs of the business

■ may be of a poor standard if those carrying it out are not highly skilled in training and communicating.

Off-the-job training

This external training usually takes place in specialist organisations, although the business may employ its own specialist training staff.

Although normally more expensive, **off-the-job** training:
- is carried out by outside specialists
- often leads to new ideas being brought into the business from outside
- is more likely to let staff being trained work at their own pace.

Cascade training

A popular recent development is trickle-down or cascade training. A number of staff are trained externally, then return to the business and train the remaining staff.

Appraisal

Most entrepreneurs recognise the value of improving employees' skills. An **appraisal system** is used to identify an individual employee's strengths and weaknesses. Appraisal involves:
- an interview between the employee and the appraiser (e.g. a supervisor)
- setting targets and identifying training needs for the employee.

KEY TERMS

Make sure you understand these terms before moving on!
- training
- induction training
- on-the-job
- off-the-job
- appraisal system

QUICK TEST

1. Tick the correct column to show whether the following are characteristics of Internal or External training.

	Internal	External
a) Usually less costly	☐	☐
b) Specialist trainers will be employed	☐	☐
c) Devoted solely to the needs of the firm	☐	☐

2. In most appraisal systems, the person being appraised is i_____ to identify any t_____ n_____ and to set t_____.

3. Identify two influences on the training offered by an organisation.

Theories on motivating staff

Why is motivation important?

Most employers accept that their staff can contribute valuable ideas, make decisions, solve problems, and take on extra responsibilities. **If employees are motivated, they will be more likely to achieve business goals**.

Abraham Maslow

This psychologist identified five human needs people wanted to satisfy. As one set of needs was satisfied, it would stop acting as a motivator, but the individual would then be motivated by the next set of needs.

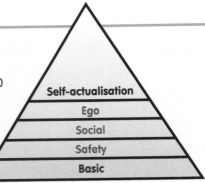

Names for the need	Meaning	Relevance to business
Self-actualisation needs	**The need to fulfil your potential**	Employers allow staff to work at what they are good at, and to organise their work in the ways they wish to do it.
Ego (for esteem) needs	**The need to be valued**	Rewards if targets are met, merit pay rises, promotion; employers offer praise and acknowledge the good work of the employee.
Social needs	**The need to belong to and work in a group**	Team meetings, company magazines, staff social events; employers allow their staff to work in groups.
Safety needs	**The need to be protected**	Safe machinery; protection in employment (e.g. a contract), and protection if the employee becomes unemployed (e.g. receiving redundancy pay).
Basic needs	**Food, warmth, sleep, clothes**	Heating, toilets, canteen; employees need money to buy these 'basics' such as food, so employers must pay a living wage.

Maslow's theory suggests employers should recognise their employees have a range of different needs, and plan work to meet this range of needs.

Frederick Herzberg

Herzberg interviewed accountants and engineers, asking them to identify what made them feel 'good' and 'bad' about their jobs. As a result, he developed a **two-factor theory** of motivation based on hygiene factors and motivators:

- **Hygiene factors** include an employee's salary, and the level of job security.
- By themselves, these are not motivators, but if they are removed they act as dissatisfiers and will demotivate the employee (the 'bad feelings' about work).
- **Motivators** act as 'satisfiers': these 'good feelings' include promotion, recognition and achievement at work.
- This suggests that challenging, interesting and rewarding work will motivate and satisfy employees.
- Herzberg concluded that the **satisfiers relate to the job's content (e.g. the job itself), and dissatisfiers to the job's context (e.g. working conditions)**.
- Satisfiers motivate when present: dissatisfiers demotivate when not present.

Douglas McGregor

- McGregor's **'Theory X'** manager believes that an employee dislikes work and will avoid it if possible.
- As a result, Theory X workers must be controlled, directed and threatened with punishment if necessary to make them work.
- McGregor's **'Theory Y'** manager believes that an employee finds work as natural as play or rest.
- As a result, they are able and willing to organise, control and direct themselves, and to accept authority and responsibility.
- Control and punishment are not effective ways to get the Theory Y employee to work.

McGregor's analysis shows that **employers should treat their employees as individuals**, finding out what exactly motivates them.

KEY TERMS

Make sure you understand these terms before moving on!
- self-actualisation needs
- ego needs
- social needs
- safety needs
- basic needs
- hygiene factors
- motivators
- 'Theory X'
- 'Theory Y'

QUICK TEST

1. Tick the relevant column:

	Maslow	Herzberg	McGregor
Theory Y	☐	☐	☐
Hygiene factors	☐	☐	☐
Self-actualisation	☐	☐	☐
Ego needs	☐	☐	☐
Motivators	☐	☐	☐

2. Are these hygiene factors or motivators?

a) 'I've just received the Employee of the Month award.'

b) 'I've just received a five per cent increase in my hourly pay rate.'

Paying staff

Work and its rewards

Pay is an important motivator. It enables people to buy things (e.g. to meet Maslow's basic needs), and pay levels are one indicator of a person's job status and power.

Non-money forms of motivation include:
- **job rotation** – allowing employees to move between jobs, especially between some of the more boring ones
- **job enrichment** – the employee's job is enriched by restructuring it to increase the tasks and responsibility
- **employee participation** – e.g. in quality circles and works councils, or as worker-directors.

 Remember that pay is not the only motivator for employees.

Pay levels

Pay levels vary between occupations and between regions. Reasons for these differences include:

- the cost of living in the area – e.g. property and rents in south-east England tend to be expensive
- the nature of work – the amount of discomfort and danger influences pay levels
- the qualifications and training required – e.g. doctors have to train for many years
- supply and demand – e.g. very talented sports stars and artists receive high pay.

The minimum wage

The government has now established a minimum wage in the UK. As a result, employers should not be able to exploit their staff, who should now receive at least this minimum level.

Wages and salaries

The normal differences are:

Wages	Salaries
paid weekly	paid monthly
hourly rates often used	stated as a yearly figure
overtime often paid	overtime often not paid
associated with factories	associated with offices
usually for manual work	usually for clerical or supervisory work

Calculating pay

Flat rate system

- **Employees receive a fixed amount**, such as one-twelfth of their annual salary each month.
- This helps employers budget for the amounts due, and administration is easier.
- There is no financial incentive for employees to work harder.

Time rate system

- **Employees receive an agreed amount for each hour worked**, and may earn overtime at higher rates of pay.
- The wage bill is more difficult to budget for and to calculate, although there is a financial incentive for staff to work longer hours.

Piece rate system

- Under this 'payment by results' system, **the employee is paid for each completed item made**.
- This encourages hard work, but there may be problems of quality if employees rush their work.

Commission and bonuses

- Employees may receive commission (e.g. the sales force **being paid something for each item sold**) as part or all of their pay.
- Employees may also be awarded merit **bonuses for the quality of work done**.
- These encourage hard work but can demotivate, e.g. if the bonus or commission is difficult to achieve.

KEY TERMS

Make sure you understand these terms before moving on!

- job rotation
- job enrichment
- employee participation
- minimum wage
- flat rate
- time rate
- piece rate
- commission
- bonus

QUICK TEST

1. List three ways in which wages and salaries usually differ.
2. How does performance-related pay differ from a flat-rate system?
3. Identify one advantage of paying staff:
   a) bonuses
   b) a share of the firm's profits.

Groups in business

In the past, harsh treatment from some business owners led to the employees joining together to protect their interests. The most important role for unions today is to protect their members' rights under the law.

In recent years, two trends have been for:

- union membership to fall – reasons include a) fewer jobs in those manufacturing industries where union membership is traditionally high, and b) difficulty in recruiting union members from the expanding service sector
- unions to merge – this gives them greater bargaining power.

Craft unions
- These were the earliest unions, which supported skilled craftsmen who had learnt their trade through the unions' apprenticeship system.
- Examples include the Musicians' Union.

Industrial unions
- These grew out of the traditional heavy industries, such as steel, coal and railways.
- Examples include USDAW, a union for workers in shops and the distribution industry.

General unions
- These usually have large memberships, often from semi-skilled and unskilled occupations.
- Examples include UNISON, a general union for public sector employees.

'White-collar' unions
- These are the most recently formed unions, due to the growing numbers of people working in clerical and administrative occupations.
- Examples include teaching unions such as the National Union of Teachers.

Union aims

The main aim of a trade union is to carry out activities to support the interests of its members. It seeks to do this through:
- improving pay levels and working conditions
- protecting jobs
- offering services such as help with legal and financial matters
- being involved in decision-making in the workplace.

Structure and membership

The typical union structure is:
- national – at the Head Office, the union's Executive will decide union policy and represent the union nationally, e.g. in the media and at national wage negotiations
- regional – the union employs representatives to work at a regional level, supporting branches and providing expertise, e.g. on legal matters
- branch – union members at the workplace are often represented by a shop steward, who is unpaid.

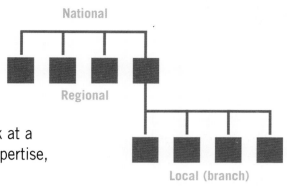

National

Regional

Local (branch)

The TUC, the CBI and other organisations

The **Trades Union Congress** (TUC) represents the views of those unions that are affiliated (joined) to it.
- As the national body for these unions, the TUC seeks to influence government policy, e.g. on political, economic and social issues.

The **Confederation of British Industry** (CBI) is to employers what the TUC is to unions. It represents employers in both the private and public sectors.

The role of **Employers' associations** includes representing employers in wage negotiations and other discussions.
Examples include:
- the National Farmers' Union
- the Road Haulage Association
- the Society of Motor Manufacturers and Traders.

KEY TERMS

Make sure you understand these terms before moving on!
- Trades Union Congress
- Confederation of British Industry
- employers' association

QUICK TEST

1. List four main aims of trade unions.

2. What aims do the TUC and CBI share?

Working together

Collective bargaining

Collective bargaining involves **negotiations between employers and unions**. These negotiations usually involve the employees' pay and their working conditions.

Collective bargaining may happen within a single company, or at a national level.

Industrial action

Sometimes disputes occur between employers and unions representing employees. A dispute may result in **industrial action**, taken by union members to persuade employers to agree to the union's wishes.

- **Overtime bans** – members refuse to work overtime, which will reduce output and may lead to orders not being met.

- **Work-to-rule** – union members are careful to follow every rule, which will reduce output.

There are different forms of industrial action

- **Go-slow** – members carry out their work more slowly than normal, but still work within their contract.

- **Picketing** – union members stand outside the firm to persuade their fellow employees not to attend work.

- **Strikes** – union members withdraw their labour by refusing to go to work.

- **Sit-ins** – union members occupy the firm's buildings to publicise their protest and persuade managers to meet their demands.

The effects of industrial action

Employers may find:

- **customers are lost** – loss of production leads to loss of sales, and customers look elsewhere for another supplier
- **cash flow becomes a problem** – lower sales means lower revenue, and a business facing industrial action may also find it difficult to raise finance if its reputation suffers because of the action
- **low employee morale** – industrial action leads to poor industrial relations, which will affect the quality of employees' work and their relationship with the employer.

Settling disputes

Managers and those employees in dispute will want to end it. **ACAS** – the Advisory, Conciliation and Arbitration Service – tries to **improve industrial relations** by offering:

- a **conciliation** service – an ACAS official will discuss the dispute with both groups
- an **arbitration** service – the groups in dispute agree to accept the ruling of an independent third party (provided by ACAS) who listens to both sides and then states how the dispute will be settled
- information and advice – ACAS has a number of information centres to help people with enquiries about employment law.

Employees, with the support of their unions, may take a complaint to an **industrial tribunal**.

- The tribunal can arrange for an employee who has been dismissed unfairly to be reinstated (re-employed) at work.
- It may also award monetary compensation to employees who have been treated unfairly.

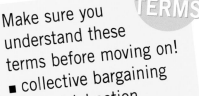

Make sure you understand these terms before moving on!
- collective bargaining
- industrial action
- ACAS
- conciliation
- arbitration
- industrial tribunal

QUICK TEST

1. What is the purpose of collective bargaining?
2. List six different forms of industrial action.
3. The three ways ACAS seeks to improve industrial relations and solve disputes are through offering a c_____ service, an a_____ service and by giving general a_____.

Practice questions

Use the questions to test your progress.
Check your answers on page 94.

1. List **three** key aspects of a company's Human Resources function.

   ....
   ....
   ....

2. People selected for interview are put on:
   a) an account ☐
   b) an agenda ☐
   c) a short list ☐
   d) a payroll ☐

3. The details of a new full-time employee's work are shown in the:
   a) final accounts ☐
   b) contract of employment ☐
   c) job description ☐
   d) person specification ☐

4. Where should these be placed in Maslow's hierarchy?
   a) 'Employee of the Month' award ....
   b) staff social event ....
   c) rest breaks ....
   d) guards being replaced on machinery...

5. List the main stages in training.

   ....
   ....

6. Merchant Ltd has an induction scheme for new starters. It also offers both on-the-job and off-the-job training for existing staff.

   a) i) Identify **one** advantage to the company as a result of recruiting staff from outside.

   ....

   ii) What factors will influence Merchant Ltd's success at recruiting staff from outside?

   ....
   ....

   b) i) Name **three** items likely to be included in Merchant Ltd's induction programme.

   ....
   ....

   ii) State **two** advantages to the company of having induction programmes.

   ....
   ....

   c) Suggest **two** reasons why Merchant Ltd's staff may prefer off-the-job training.

   ....
   ....

7. Osborne Ltd is a manufacturing company making components used in cars and vans. The directors are planning to move their warehouse from its present location to a new site about 30 km away. Staff working in the warehouse are upset about the proposed move, and have contacted their union representatives. The trade unions at Osborne Ltd have recently negotiated a 'no-strike' agreement, in return for higher-than-average pay increases for their members.

a) What is the role of trade unions concerning the possible move of the warehouse?

....

....

b) In addition to the roles of the union outlined above, explain **one** other likely area of trade union involvement at Osborne Ltd.

....

....

c) Identify and explain the nature of **two** other forms of industrial action the unions could advise their members to undertake.

....

....

....

d) Outline the role of ACAS in resolving industrial disputes.

....

....

....

8. This is a job advert for a shop assistant:

> # WANTED
> ## Full-time SHOP ASSISTANT
> We are looking for an outgoing young man with a pleasant personality, who gets on well with members of the public.
> We offer pleasant working conditions and a good rate of pay. Overtime is possible.
> Full training will be given to the successful applicant.

a) Suggest **one** criticism of the advert's content.

....

....

b) Identify **three** other items of information you would expect to see in the advert.

....

....

....

c) i) Identify the payment system mentioned in the advert.

....

....

ii) Describe an alternative payment system suitable for this position.

....

....

....

....

How well did you do? X 1-2 Start again   3-4 Getting there   5-6 Good work   7-8 Excellent! ✓

53

Finance for business

Why is finance needed?

All organisations need finance:

- to start in business – to do this, they need assets which they must buy

- to survive – the cash inflows of a business must match their cash outflows, otherwise the business will not be able to pay its way

- to grow – a business needs finance to buy more assets and to meet expenses so that it can expand

Sources for the private sector

Internal sources
- The main source of day-to-day cash comes from sales.
- Keeping profits in the business, using the cash from these profits to invest in business development.
- The owners can use **trade credit**, delaying paying their bills to save cash.
- They can reduce stock levels to free the cash 'tied up' in these stocks.
- Businesses can sell any surplus assets they no longer need.

External sources
- The savings of the owner, and/or **borrowing** from family and friends, are possible sources for sole traders and partners.
- Limited companies can issue **shares**.
- Banks arrange short-term borrowing such as **overdrafts**.
- **Loans** are also available from banks (and other financial institutions), are longer-term finance than overdrafts, and often have fixed repayment amounts.
- The business can sell its debts by 'factoring' them to a specialist firm.
- **Government grants** may be available, e.g. when setting up business in certain regions.
- Hire purchase and leasing are possible sources of extra finance.

Sources for the public sector

- Public corporations get their finance through government grants from tax collected, and by borrowing from the Treasury.
- Local authority undertakings are also funded through government grants, through collecting taxes and rates from local people and businesses, and by running revenue-making businesses such as local leisure centres.

Shares

These are the main source of long-term finance available to limited companies. Shares are sold to people who become shareholders – owners – of the company.

- A PLC is able to advertise its shares for sale to the general public.
- A private limited company (ltd) must sell its shares privately.

Companies usually issue **ordinary shares**.

- Their owners can vote at the company's annual general meeting.
- The dividend received by the shareholders varies according to the amount of profits left.
- The owners receive their dividend after all other debts and people have been paid.
- The owners are last to have their capital repaid if the company stops trading.

Debentures

Debentures are loans made to companies. They differ from shares in that:

- the debenture holders are lenders to, not owners of, the company
- these lenders receive a fixed rate of interest rather than dividends
- if the interest is not paid, the debenture holders may take legal action to recover their debts.

Choosing the finance

- The **type of project** for which the finance is needed is an important influence, e.g. whether it is a long-term or short-term project.
- The **nature of the business** is a key influence – some businesses have little choice (e.g. those in the public sector), and small firms and those businesses in high-risk areas may find their sources are limited.

KEY TERMS

Make sure you understand these terms before moving on!

- trade credit
- borrowing
- shares
- overdraft
- loan
- government grant
- ordinary shares
- debenture

QUICK TEST

1. List three reasons why businesses need finance.
2. State two differences between being a shareholder and being a debenture holder.
3. Name one:
   a) short-term source of finance
   b) medium-term source of finance
   c) long-term source of finance.

Financial records in business

The role of financial accounting

By keeping financial records, businesses can:
- collect financial information from original documents such as invoices and bank statements
- record financial transactions in the accounts
- analyse this financial information, e.g. by using accounting ratios
- make decisions on financial matters.

The Trading, Profit and Loss Account

- This shows the business's **financial performance**.
- **Profit** is the difference between its **revenue** (e.g. from sales) and its **expenses**, such as the cost of any raw materials, wages and salaries, and selling and distribution costs.
- The trading account calculates the business's **gross profit**, the difference between its turnover and what these sales have cost the business.
- The profit and loss account is used to deduct all other expenses from the gross profit, leaving the **net profit** for the business.

	£
sales	40 000
less cost of sales	15 000
gross profit	25 000
less expenses	5 000
net profit	20 000

The Balance Sheet

- This shows the business's **financial position** by listing its **assets** (what it owns) and **liabilities** (what it owes).

	£	£
fixed assets		200 000
current assets	75 000	
current liabilities	25 000	
		50 000
		250 000
capital and reserves		250 000

The Cash Flow Statement

Many businesses have to produce a **Cash Flow Statement**. The purpose of this statement is to summarise the cash inflows and outflows that have taken place during the trading period. It includes cash movements from:
- trading activities
- buying and selling assets
- receiving or repaying long-term capital
- paying share dividends.

Published accounts

The directors of a public limited company must publish its **financial statements (final accounts)**.

This means that these accounts are available to members of the public, and also to the PLC's competitors.

The PLC will therefore normally only show in its published accounts the minimum information required by law.

A PLC will also publish supporting statements with its accounts.

These include:
- the chairman's statement, outlining the company's successes in the year
- the directors' report on the company's performance
- an auditors' report stating that the accounts have been checked by them
- a five-year summary of the company's financial performance.

KEY TERMS

Make sure you understand these terms before moving on!
- profit
- revenue
- expenses
- gross profit
- net profit
- assets
- liabilities
- Cash Flow Statement

QUICK TEST

Match each item in column A with the correct item in column B.

A	B
a) gross profit	i) list of assets and liabilities
b) cash flow statement	ii) written review of the company performance
c) balance sheet	iii) summary of cash inflows and outflows for the year
d) profit and loss account	iv) net profit
e) directors' report	v) sales less the cost of those sales

Interpreting business accounts

- Business accounts are used to record financial information.
- This financial information can then be used to judge the business's financial situation.

The users of financial information

Many **stakeholder groups** are interested in a business's financial situation.
The groups include:
- actual and potential shareholders and other investors, who want to assess **profitability**
- lenders such as creditors and banks, who want to make sure they will get their money back, and will therefore check the business's **liquidity**
- managers, who will want to assess the overall performance of the business
- employees, who are interested in how safe their jobs are
- the government, which will want to be paid VAT and other taxes
- the local community, interested in the financial success or failure of the business.

Profitability ratios

The profitability of the business measures its profit against some other figure.
- The most important measure of profitability for a business is **ROCE** – its Return On Capital Employed.
- This is calculated by measuring the profit as a percentage of capital employed in the business.
- This calculation tells the investors whether their investment is worthwhile.

Other profitability measures include:
- **net profit margin** – this measures net profit as a percentage of turnover (net sales)
- **gross profit margin** – this ratio calculates gross profit as a percentage of turnover.

 You have to distinguish between 'profit' and 'profitability'

Using ratios

The main value of using ratios is when:
- trends can be seen, by comparing the business's previous performance with past figures
- competitors' ratios are compared with those of the business.

Liquidity ratios

The liquidity of a business shows its ability to pay its debts as they become due. The business's current assets – its stocks, debtors and bank and cash balances – are compared with its current liabilities (its short-term debts). Calculating the difference between current assets and current liabilities shows the business's **working capital**.

- The **current ratio** compares the total current assets with the total current liabilities.
- This shows whether or not the business can easily pay its short-term debts.
- The **acid test** (also known as the Quick Assets ratio) takes the stock figure off the current assets, and then compares the result against the total current liabilities.

Efficiency ratios

1. Rate of stock turnover = $\dfrac{\text{cost of sales}}{\text{average stock}}$

This shows how many times stock is 'turned over' (sold) in the period.

2. Debtors' collection period = $\dfrac{\text{debtors x 365}}{\text{sales}}$

This shows how long debtors (customers buying on credit) are taking to pay the business.

3. Creditors' collection period = $\dfrac{\text{creditors x 365}}{\text{purchases}}$

This shows the length of time (in days) the business takes to pay its creditors (suppliers on credit).

KEY TERMS

Make sure you understand these terms before moving on!
- profitability
- liquidity
- ROCE
- net profit margin
- gross profit margin
- working capital
- current ratio
- acid test

QUICK TEST

1 What is the difference between 'profit' and 'profitability'?

2 Name two ratios used to measure a company's liquidity.

Costs in business

Costs

Business have many different costs. Examples include:

- wages and salaries
- raw materials
- light, heat and power
- finance costs
- maintenance
- administration

Cost behaviour

Some costs change as a business's output changes, but other costs may not be affected by these changes.

- A **variable cost** is one that **changes in direct proportion to output**.
- Popular examples are the cost of raw materials and piece-rate labour used to make the product.
- A **fixed cost** **stays the same even though output may change**.
- Examples include the rent and rates, and office salaries, paid by the business.
- This analysis is important in helping accountants make decisions, and in break-even analysis.

Standard costing

Many businesses establish what the cost of their products should be.

In doing so, they set standards for the costs of the different items making up the product.

- The actual costs of making the product are then paid out and recorded.
- The actual cost of materials, labour and overheads is then compared with the standard ('expected') cost: these differences are called variances.
- The variances can be studied to see why the difference has occurred.

Direct costs

■ A **direct cost** can be **linked directly to a product**: for example, the main raw material used in making the product. These are some of the direct costs of a car:

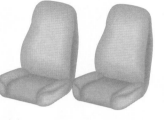

driver and passenger seat

driver's wheel

tyres

gear stick

windscreen

Indirect costs

■ An **indirect cost** is one that **cannot be traced directly to a particular product**: e.g. canteen and office costs. Indirect costs are usually called **overheads**.
■ The distinction between direct and indirect costs is important when accountants try to calculate the full cost of making individual products.
■ It is easy to calculate the product's direct costs, but indirect costs have to be **apportioned** – shared out – between the different products.

KEY TERMS

Make sure you understand these terms before moving on!
■ variable cost
■ fixed cost
■ direct cost
■ indirect cost
■ overhead
■ apportioning

QUICK TEST

1 State whether these costs are likely to be
   i) direct or indirect, and ii) fixed or variable:
   a) Steel used to make a car body
   b) Office rent
   c) The pay of a person assembling parts
      on one particular product line
   d) An accountant's salary

2 Indirect costs are also known as
   o_____, which have to be
   a_____ between the different
   products made by the business.

3 What is the purpose of standard costing?

Breaking even in business

Break-even

- The break-even point for a business is where total revenue is the same as total costs. At this point the business is making neither a profit nor a loss.
- Break-even analysis separates costs into fixed or variable types, and is valuable because it calculates the point at which the business starts making a profit.

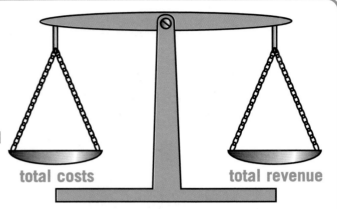

total costs   total revenue

Constructing the chart

A company has £100 000 fixed costs. The selling price of its product is £30, and the variable cost is £10. The product's output and sales are expected to reach 10 000.

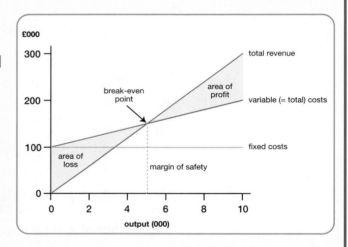

The fixed cost line
- This is plotted against the '£100 000' point on the vertical '£' axis.
- It stays parallel with the horizontal 'output' axis, because **fixed costs do not change with output**.

The variable cost line
- This line climbs at a rate of £10 per unit of output.
- It is often plotted from the point at which the fixed cost line meets the vertical axis.
- In such cases, the variable cost line also acts as the total cost line.

The sales line
- This climbs from where the axes meet, at a rate of £30 for each unit of output
- The line represents the **total revenue line**.
- When this line meets the variable (total) cost line, this shows the **break-even point**.
- The **margin of safety** can now be calculated: this is the gap between the expected output and the break-even output, and shows **how many units sales can fall by before the business starts making a loss**.
- The triangle formed to the left of the break-even point represents the **area of loss**, and the triangle to the right of it the **area of profit**.
- The profit or loss at any output can now be read from the chart, both as output and as revenue.

Calculating the break-even point

The normal method used to calculate the break-even point is:

total fixed costs
unit contribution

('**contribution**' is **the difference between selling price and variable costs**).

We can re-use the figures from our break-even chart
- Selling price £30 less variable cost £10 = contribution £20

- $\frac{£100\ 000}{£20}$ = 5000 units (this break-even point can be seen on the chart)
- Proof: at 5000 units
  total revenue = 5000 x £30 = £150 000
  variable costs = £50 000 (5000 x £10) + fixed costs £100 000
  total costs = £150 000

 Knowing how to calculate the break-even point allows you to check any chart you have to draw.

Limitations of break-even analysis

- The break-even chart is a clear and simple planning tool that can help managers make decisions, e.g. if costs or revenue figures change.
- However, variable costs do not always change in proportion to output (e.g. bulk-buying discounts, or overtime paid to manufacturing employees).
- The business may also set different selling prices in different markets.
- Break-even analysis is difficult to use if the business makes more than one product.

KEY TERMS

Make sure you understand these terms before moving on!
- total cost line
- total revenue line
- break-even point
- margin of safety
- area of loss
- area of profit
- contribution

QUICK TEST

1. An organisation's break-even point is where its t_____ c_____ are the same as its t_____ r_____.

2. A company selling a single product has these costs: fixed costs £35 000, variable costs £8 per unit and selling price £15 per unit. It expects to make and sell 8 000 units. Calculate:

   a) the break-even point in units and in revenue

   b) the margin of safety.

Budgeting in business

Managers budget for various reasons:

■ their budget makes them plan for the future resources they will need

■ it helps them check their progress through comparing their actual results with those they had budgeted for

■ this means that budgets can help control expenditure (this is known as *budgetary control*)

■ the budget gives the manager the authority to spend what is in the budget.

Why budget?

One of the benefits of budgeting is that it makes managers work together when designing their budgets, because their budgets are often linked. For example:

■ the sales budget influences figures in the production budget
■ the production budget affects the raw materials purchases budget
■ this purchases budget is one of the main influences on the cash budget.

Budgeting is a motivating activity, especially when a manager meets the 'targets' or objectives set by the budget.

Preparing budgets

A budget is a financial plan. The **budget committee** controls the preparation of the business budgets. The procedures for preparing the budgets are usually written down in a **budget manual**.

The two main groups of budgets are:

■ **operating budgets** – cash, stocks, sales, purchasing and the other budgets that come from the main operations of the business.

■ **summary budgets** – these are budgeted final accounts:
■ budgeted profit and loss
■ budgeted balance sheet
■ budgeted cash flow statement.

 Learn the definition of 'budget'.

Cash budgeting

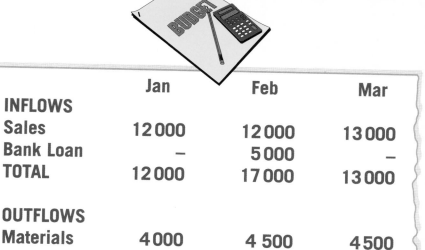

	Jan	Feb	Mar
INFLOWS			
Sales	12000	12000	13000
Bank Loan	–	5000	–
TOTAL	12000	17000	13000
OUTFLOWS			
Materials	4000	4500	4500
Labour	3000	3200	3200

The main **sources of cash** are:
- capital from the owner(s)
- loans from banks and other lenders
- cash from sales
- trade credit from suppliers
- profits retained in the business.

The main **uses of cash** are:
- buying assets
- paying expenses
- paying back loan interest
- paying taxes
- allowing credit to customers.

One problem with the cash budget is that it is only an estimate. The managers will therefore need to check the actual cash flow that is taking place to ensure the business has enough cash to meet its bills.

KEY TERMS

Make sure you understand these terms before moving on!
- budgetary control
- budget committee
- budget manual
- operating budget
- summary budget

QUICK TEST

1. Identify three benefits that come from budgeting.

2. Tick the relevant column:

	Source of cash	Use of cash
a) paying an electricity bill	☐	☐
b) taking out a bank loan	☐	☐
c) receiving credit from a supplier	☐	☐
d) receiving cash from goods sold	☐	☐
e) buying a delivery van	☐	☐

Practice questions

Use the questions to test your progress.
Check your answers on page 94–5.

1. Which of these will a company's accounts department be responsible for?

   Planning production runs ☐   Stock control ☐
   Storing finished goods ☐   Planning an advertising campaign ☐
   Calculating financial ratios ☐   Attracting good publicity ☐
   Appointing staff ☐   Preparing financial statements ☐

2. The variable costs of a business change according to which of the following:
   a) taxation ☐
   b) cash flow ☐
   c) break even ☐
   d) output? ☐

3. Which of these will be used in producing a break-even chart?
   a) a balance sheet ☐
   b) a cash flow forecast ☐
   c) production figures ☐
   d) an organisation chart ☐

4. Businesses that supply on credit are known as:
   a) debtors ☐
   b) creditors ☐
   c) dividends ☐
   d) mortgages? ☐

5. Which of these are financial statements?

   a profit and loss account ☐   an inspection schedule ☐
   a contract of employment ☐   a cash flow statement ☐
   a job description ☐   a stock control chart ☐
   a production planning schedule ☐   a person specification ☐

6. Identify and explain the importance of **two** factors that help the owners of a business decide on their sources of finance.

   ....
   ....
   ....

7. A company's production manager has forecast that 200 units of its product will be made in a week. Production costs are expected to be £51 000. The accountant has calculated that these costs will rise to £52 000 if the company makes 220 units.

   a) Calculate the average cost of production of the 200 units.

   ....

   b) Calculate the variable cost of the 20 extra units.

   ....

   c) Explain why these two figures are different.

   ....
   ....

8. A company's final accounts include these figures.

Trading, profit and loss account in £000		Balance sheet in £000	
Sales	600	Capital employed	1500
Cost of sales	450	Stock	50
Gross profit	150	Other current assets	100
Net profit	30	Current liabilities	100

a) Calculate suitable profitability and liquidity ratios.

....
....
....
....

b) Comment on your results.

....
....
....
....

c) State any other information you need to interpret your results more fully.

....
....
....
....

9. Hash Patel runs his own business, printing and selling T-shirts. He pays £3000 rent a year, and pays a part-time assistant a yearly salary of £5000. Hash has calculated that each T-shirt costs 80p to buy and 20p for the printing process. He plans to sell his T-shirts to local shops for £3 each. Hash hopes to print and sell 6000 T-shirts a year.

a) Calculate how many T-shirts Hash must buy and sell in a year to break even.

....
....

b) Construct Hash's break-even chart on a separate piece of paper.
From the chart, identify:
i) the break-even point

....

ii) Hash's break-even revenue

....

iii) the profit or loss Hash expects to make in the year

....

iv) any margin of safety for Hash

....

How well did you do?   X   1-2 Start again   3-4 Getting there   5-7 Good work   8-10 Excellent!   ✓

67

Production in business

Entrepreneurs need to choose the most efficient way to make their products. Their choice is influenced by the type of product they are making, and the output they require.

Methods of production

Job production is when a business makes a single, one-off product.

- Examples include items constructed such as motorways, ships, and house extensions.
- The job is often built by skilled labour working to the customer's requirements.
- Since only one item is made, the business may not gain economies of scale.

Batch production is when more than one item at a time is made, with each batch of products being finished before the next batch (of different products) is started.

- Examples include shoes and clothing.
- Batch production is often used to make items which have a range of styles or sizes.
- The number made per batch can be based on the demand for the finished items.

Mass production (also known as flow or continuous) is when identical items are made on a production line. The product moves from one stage of production straight to the next.

- Examples include cars and consumer durables, canned foodstuffs and drinks.
- Staff and machines specialise in producing items sold on the **mass market**.
- Production is often highly automated, with machines replacing manual labour.

Lean production

Mass production has been criticised because

- employees can become easily bored
- machines and labour are over-specialised.

Lean production methods can overcome these drawbacks. This term refers to the ways that are now used to improve the efficiency of production.

It is often associated with **just-in-time** stock control, **cell production** and the **Kaizen** system.

Just-in-time stockholding

This seeks to cut stockholding costs.

- This can be achieved if the business operates with no buffer (reserve) stocks.

- It runs down its stocks of raw materials, work-in-progress and finished goods.

- The business needs efficient ordering systems, and must have reliable suppliers.

Cell production

Businesses use cell production to overcome problems of low worker morale.

- The production line is divided into separate units (cells), each making an identifiable part of the finished product.

- Employees are more motivated, which increases output.

Kaizen

This Japanese term means 'continuous improvement'. It is based on improvement through investing in people and their ideas rather than in new technology or equipment.

- Groups are set up to improve their own efficiency.

- They achieve this by discussing production issues, then suggesting and implementing solutions.

KEY TERMS

Make sure you understand these terms before moving on!
- job production
- batch production
- mass production
- production line
- lean production
- just-in-time
- cell production
- Kaizen

QUICK TEST

❶ Tick the correct column:

	Job	Batch	Mass
a) Cans of paint	☐	☐	☐
b) A factory extension	☐	☐	☐
c) Shoes, size 7	☐	☐	☐
d) Televisions	☐	☐	☐
e) The Channel Tunnel	☐	☐	☐

❷ State one advantage and one disadvantage of mass production.

Economies of scale

Large-scale business

The costs of a business are either fixed or variable. As output goes up, the fixed costs stay the same. Although total costs will still rise, the average cost per unit will fall. **The reason is that the fixed costs are spread over a larger output**.
- Economies of scale occur when the average costs of the business fall.
- This means the cost per unit will be lower.
- **Lower unit costs make the business more price competitive**.

With economies of scale, remember total costs increase but the average cost per unit falls.

Internal economies of scale

These economies are gained by a business through its own growth.
The main internal economies of scale are:
- **purchasing economies** – a large business can buy in bulk, paying cheaper prices for its materials and other purchases
- **marketing economies** – marketing and advertising costs are spread over much greater output
- **financial economies** – large businesses often receive loans at lower interest rates, and find it easier to obtain these loans
- **technical economies** – a large business can buy more efficient machinery, which may replace its labour and help the business save these costs
- **managerial economies** – the larger business can employ efficient specialist managers, which will improve its decision-making
- **risk-bearing economies** – larger firms are more likely to diversify into different markets, and are not so badly affected if sales slump in one market.

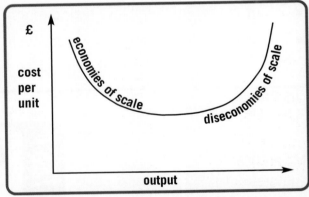

External economies of scale

These economies are gained by all businesses in an industry. The main ones are:
- **economies of concentration** – where an industry is located in one area, that area develops a skilled labour force, specialist training and support services for the industry
- **economies of information** – businesses in the same area may work together to obtain and share market information, and the costs of research and development
- **economies of reputation** – the good reputation of an area will help all businesses located in that area sell their products.

Diseconomies of scale

At some point, the business will discover that its unit costs start to increase again. These are **diseconomies of scale**. These diseconomies occur because the business cannot continue for ever becoming more cost-effective and more efficient. Causes include having poor:

- communication – as a business grows, the number of levels in the hierarchy increases, which slows communication down
- morale and motivation – the greater 'distance' between top and bottom in the hierarchy can leave employees with a 'them and us' feeling, which can affect their work effort
- co-ordination – managers in larger businesses often find it more difficult to keep all functions working together effectively.

Preventing diseconomies

Problem	Possible action
communication	improve communication systems control the amount of communication train staff in good communication practices de-layer (reduce the number of levels in the hierarchy)
morale and motivation	use job rotation and job enrichment delegate more responsibility to staff
co-ordination	improve communication de-layer increase spans of control

KEY TERMS

Make sure you understand these terms before moving on!

- purchasing economy
- marketing economy
- financial economy
- technical economy
- managerial economy
- risk-bearing economy
- economy of concentration
- economy of information
- economy of reputation
- diseconomy of scale

QUICK TEST

1. Name the relevant economy of scale:
   a) a cheaper rate of interest on a bank loan
   b) a discount off raw materials when a large order is placed
   c) a specialist accountant is employed
   d) a business starts selling its products in a new market.

2. What is the main difference between internal and external economies of scale?

Productivity

What is productivity?

Production is the output of a business. **Productivity takes this output, and measures it against the inputs used to create it**. These inputs are the four factors of production – land, labour, capital and enterprise. Productivity is often measured against staff, being stated as productivity or output 'per employee'.

- Output per employee measures what a person produces in a set period of time.
- This is easy to calculate for manufacturing businesses, but less easy for businesses that provide a service.

Productivity is important because it affects the costs of the business, and therefore its competitiveness.

 Make sure you can distinguish between 'production' and 'productivity'.

Improving productivity

There are two main ways to improve the productivity of a business:
- the same inputs are used more efficiently to produce a higher output
- the same output is made, but with fewer inputs.

The practical ways this is done are to:
- buy more modern equipment
- train staff to be more efficient
- improve employee motivation, e.g. through higher pay or greater involvement.

A popular way of increasing productivity in recent years has been to substitute capital for labour.
- This occurs when a business invests in labour-saving machinery.
- The machinery is often more productive than the employees it replaces.
- The business can now cut its labour force, and save costs by doing so.

Full capacity

If a business's resources are working at maximum output, it is producing at **full capacity**. Although full or near-full capacity means the business is operating efficiently, it can cause problems for:
- staff – e.g. high stress levels
- machines and equipment – greater use can mean more frequent breakdowns.

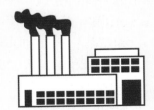

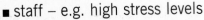

Surplus capacity

If a business has surplus capacity, it may try to get rid of this. Ways include:
- not replacing staff when they leave
- moving to smaller premises
- selling assets that the business no longer needs.

Capital intensity

Capital intensity measures how much a business depends on machinery and equipment, compared with depending on labour.
- **Capital intensive businesses often make products sold in mass production markets**.
- Businesses in these markets can afford to buy and use expensive capital equipment.

CAD and CAM

Many businesses use advanced equipment to improve productivity.
- Computer-aided design (CAD) packages are used to create cost-effective designs for new products, or to re-style existing products.
- Computer-aided manufacture (CAM) uses robots and other hi-tech equipment to produce output efficiently and reliably.

Using technology

Although investing in new technology may make a business more productive:
- it is expensive to invest in new technology
- employees may resent changes in their work practices when the new technology is introduced.

KEY TERMS

Make sure you understand these terms before moving on!
- productivity
- full capacity
- surplus capacity
- capital intensity
- computer-aided design
- computer-aided manufacture

QUICK TEST

❶ Productivity measures the o_____ of a business against the i_____ used to produce it. It is often stated as 'productivity p____ e_____'. Increasing productivity makes a business more c_____, because its u_____ c_____ of production f_____.

❷ What is the difference between CAD and CAM?

Quality and stock control

Quality

Quality assurance
- **makes sure that quality standards are set**
- sets these standards throughout the business.

Quality control
- **checks that the quality standards are being maintained**
- tries to stop problems occurring in the first place
- identifies defects in products before these are sent to the customer.

Total Quality Management (TQM)
- **seeks to 'get it right first time' and to 'get it more right next time'**
- is concerned with giving full customer satisfaction
- believes that high quality standards will reduce costs (e.g. costs of inspection)
- is closely linked with Kaizen ('continuous improvement') and the use of quality circles.

Stock control

Businesses hold different types of stock:
- administration stock – e.g. stationery used by the office staff
- production stock – e.g. spare parts for machines
- products – finished goods items ready for delivery, and (for a manufacturer) raw materials in stores plus any work in progress in the factory.

Stock costs

The business has costs of holding stock. This encourages staff to keep stock levels as low as possible. **The risk of doing this is being out of stock.** Costs of being out of stock include:
- idle time for the employees, which must be paid for
- lost production in the factory
- lost customers and poor reputation through failing to meet orders.

To avoid these costs, managers may keep stock levels high. High stock levels have these costs:
- **money is 'tied up' in the stock**, and cannot be used elsewhere in the business
- storage costs are higher
- the stock may become out-of-date, or may deteriorate
- there may be a greater risk of theft.

The **Just-in-time** (JIT) system **seeks to minimise costs** by:
- making finished goods just in time to be sent to the buyer
- receiving raw materials just in time for production
- making part of the finished product just in time for it to be used in the next production process.

If JIT is to work successfully, few errors can be made. JIT therefore often operates as part of a **total quality management** (TQM) system.

Optimum stock

Managers will calculate the **optimum stock** level.
This is the level that reduces costs to a minimum.
They take into account:
- the **reorder level** – the stock level at which a new order will be made
- the **minimum stock** level – the 'buffer' stock, which, in a 'just-in-time' system, is at or near zero
- the **maximum stock** – the highest level of stock
- the **reorder quantity** – the most economical number to order.

An **economic order quantity** (EOQ) can be calculated by comparing the costs of holding stock with the savings available through bulk-buying.

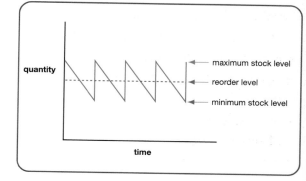

KEY TERMS

Make sure you understand these terms before moving on!
- just-in-time
- total quality management
- optimum stock
- reorder level
- minimum stock
- maximum stock
- reorder quantity
- economic order quantity

QUICK TEST

❶ Costs of holding high stocks include large s_____ costs, and the risk of the stock becoming o____ o___ d____ . The costs of holding low stocks include the risk of being o____ o___ s_____ , and therefore losing c_____.

❷ Explain the following: a) TQM
b) JIT
c) EOQ

Practice questions

Use the questions to test your progress. Check your answers on page 95.

1. The job method of production is used to make:
   a) newspapers ☐
   b) bridges ☐
   c) televisions ☐
   d) vacuum cleaners ☐

2. Which of the following form part of the production function?

   Undertaking quality control ☐   Producing questionnaires ☐
   Measuring productivity ☐   Inducting new staff ☐
   Producing invoices ☐   Undertaking personal selling ☐

3. Link these terms with their descriptions.

   a) Lean production   i) The level to which stock must fall to trigger a new order
   b) Just-in-time   ii) The number of stock items ordered
   c) Buffer stock   iii) An approach used to minimise waste and overcome some of the problems of mass production
   d) Reorder level   iv) A system for delivering more stock to production just before it runs out
   e) Reorder quantity   v) A check to see if quality standards are being met
   f) Quality control   vi) A 'reserve' stock level held in case of problems

4. a) Link these terms with their description and with the most appropriate illustration.

Economy	Description	Illustration
1) Concentration	a) specialist managers	i) Cornish pasties
2) Purchasing	b) good name of the area	ii) joint research venture
3) Reputation	c) specialist advertising	iii) skilled labour force
4) Technical	d) using specialist machinery	iv) discounts on raw materials
5) Marketing	e) cheaper money	v) advertising agency employed
6) Information	f) industry located in a limited area	vi) HRM manager
7) Managerial	g) businesses share research	vii) paying lower interest rates
8) Financial	h) buying in bulk	viii) CAD/CAM machines

   b) Identify the external economies of scale in the above list.

   ....

5. Supercuddle Ltd is a company producing toys for a specialist, collectors' market. Some toys are made individually by hand, and others are produced as 'limited editions'.
   a) Identify the most appropriate production method used

   i) to make toys individually

   ....

   ii) to make 'limited edition' toys

   ....

   b) Give **three** reasons why Supercuddle Ltd may find it cheaper to produce the limited edition toys.

   ....
   ....
   ....

6. These are the possible output figures for Watchit Ltd, a company making and selling computer screens.

Expected yearly sales (000)	Unit cost price (£)	Unit selling price (£)
5	45	60
6	44	57
7	42	55
8	40	52
9	41	50

a) How do these figures show that Watchit Ltd gains from economies of scale?

....

....

....

b) Suggest **two** economies of scale which you would expect this company to have. Give reasons for your choice.

....

....

....

c) The directors have decided to sell their screens for £52 each. Explain why you think they have chosen this figure.

....

....

....

7. Go-Low Plc is a company that produces various low-calorie food agents for use in sweet foodstuffs such as chocolate and ice cream. The low-calorie product is used as a sugar substitute. Go-Low Plc uses both mass (flow-line) and batch production methods to make its products. The company is aware of the importance of good quality systems. The directors have introduced a Total Quality Management (TQM) system in the company.

a) i) Explain, with an example of each, the difference between batch production and mass production.

....

....

....

....

ii) Compare the suitability of each of these production methods for making low-calorie food agents (artificial sweeteners).

....

....

....

....

b) i) Explain the meaning of 'Total Quality Management'.

....

....

....

ii) How might this system apply to a company such as Go-Low PLC?

....

....

How well did you do?   X   1-2 **Start again**   3-4 **Getting there**   5-6 **Good work**   all 7 **Excellent!**   ✓

Marketing in business

Markets

A **market** consists of **people – buyers and sellers – who are trading in a product**. This market may be local (e.g. a street market), national (the mass market) or international. Markets can be classified as:

- consumer markets – goods and services bought by the general public
- industrial markets – machinery and equipment used in business, and business-related services (e.g. delivery, security).

Marketing

Marketing is needed because people, businesses and advanced economies all specialise. The various goods and services supplied need to be sold. A business needs to discover:

- what to make and sell
- how many to make and sell
- who to sell to
- how to encourage these people to buy
- how much to charge for what is sold.

The marketing department

The role of the marketing department is to make sure that **the demands of its customers are met by what is being made**. If the marketing department achieves this, it will meet customer wishes and help the business make a profit.

Marketing planning

This helps the marketing department achieve its objectives. **The existing position can be analysed** using a **SWOT analysis**. This analyses:

- S – the business's present strengths
- W – and weaknesses
- O – its market opportunities
- T – and the external threats it faces.

Market segmentation

A market is segmented by **dividing it into different parts (segments)**. When this is carried out, the business may concentrate on one, several or all the different segments. If the business concentrates on one segment only, this is its **niche market**. These markets are normally for specialist, or limited demand, items.

Market segmentation helps the marketing department to understand its market. It allows the business to target:
- the product in each segment by establishing its USP (**Unique Selling Point**), the feature that distinguishes this product from others
- its advertising and other forms of promotion in the segment.

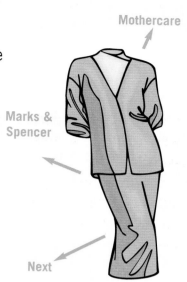

Mothercare

Marks & Spencer

Next

Ways to segment

- Sex – marketers target certain products (e.g. some drinks) at either men or women.

- Age – e.g. fashion clothing and music aimed at the youth market.

- Ethnicity – people with different backgrounds have different wants, e.g. religious beliefs and cultural tastes regarding food.

There are different ways to segment a market.

- Population – its size and distribution varies, and regional tastes also differ.

- Income and social class – e.g. 'luxury' goods and high-price cars aimed at wealthier consumers.

- Lifestyle – e.g. sports and exercise goods and services.

Make sure you understand these terms before moving on!
- market
- SWOT analysis
- niche market
- market segmentation
- unique selling point

QUICK TEST

1. List four different ways to segment a consumer market.
2. The 'marketing mix' consists of: p_____, p_____, d_____ (or p_____) and p_____.
3. State one possible strength, weakness, opportunity and threat for a business you have studied.

Market research

Getting information

The role of **market research** is to **get information about the market(s) in which the business operates**. This is one part of marketing research, which also includes research into:
- the product – e.g. its price and its packaging
- the promotion – e.g. if the best advertising media are being used.

Secondary data

This comes from **existing sources that have already been published**.
It is known as **desk research**, because the information can be
obtained by sitting at a desk. Information from inside the
business can be used, for example:
- sales and production figures
- the cost of marketing campaigns
- selling and distribution costs.

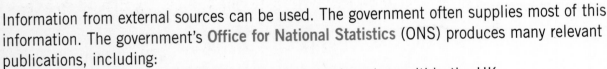

Information from external sources can be used. The government often supplies most of this information. The government's **Office for National Statistics** (ONS) produces many relevant publications, including:
- Regional Trends – e.g. population movements taking place within the UK
- Social Trends – e.g. how consumer spending is changing
- Economic Trends – this summarises the changes taking place in the economy.

Published information is available from many other sources, e.g.:
- banks
- chambers of commerce
- the TUC and the CBI
- professional associations
- newspapers.

Comparing primary and secondary

- primary data is obtained exclusively for the business
- it is therefore **more appropriate for the needs of the business**
- because it needs collecting 'from scratch', it is **much more costly than secondary data** and takes longer to collect
- although secondary data is cheaper and quicker to obtain, it has the major disadvantage that it is not designed for the needs of the business.

Primary data

This data does not already exist. It is obtained from research into the market.

Research used to obtain primary data may be either quantitative or qualitative.

- **Quantitative research summarises the findings in the form of figures**.
  For example, in a survey, 'closed' questions such as 'how many ...?' or 'which of these ...?' will be asked.
- **Qualitative research studies consumer's behaviour**.
- In a survey 'open' questions will be set, e.g. to find out reasons for buying, and opinions about the product.

Interviews

These take place either face-to-face (usually for products in consumer markets) or by telephone (often for industrial market products).

- Information can be obtained quickly, and the interviewer can explain questions if necessary.
- **Questionnaires** have to be designed carefully, and it is an expensive method of collecting data.

Postal surveys

These are popular alternatives to personal interviews.

- This is normally less expensive than conducting interviews, and a wide geographical area can be sampled.
- The postal survey may have only a low response rate.

Consumer panels

These groups of people meet to discuss the market or product being researched.

- Different types of panel can be used: e.g. product panels obtain views on new products, and buying panels review buying habits.

Observation

The actions of consumers in the market-place are observed, e.g. using cameras placed in shops.

- This gives more objective evidence.
- Observing people behave in the way they do will not explain their behaviour.

KEY TERMS

Make sure you understand these terms before moving on!

- market research
- desk research
- Office for National Statistics
- quantitative research
- qualitative research
- questionnaire

QUICK TEST

1. Popular ways of collecting primary data are to use f_____ t___ f_____ i_____, t_____ s_____ and p_____ s_____.

2. List three sources of secondary data, other than the UK government.

Product

The product mix

Many businesses sell more than one product. The range of products they sell is known as the **'product mix'**. The product mix for any business is influenced by the number of market segments it sells in.

The Boston Matrix

The **Boston Matrix** ('Boston Box') is used to analyse the product mix.

- Stars – have **a high market share in a fast-growing market**, but need much investment to turn them into Cash Cows.
- Cash Cows – **a high market share in mature markets**, these are the business's most valuable products.
- Problem Children – **a low market share in a high-growth market**, needing further investment to be successful.
- Dogs – **a low market share in a low-growth market**, and are unprofitable (or loss-making).

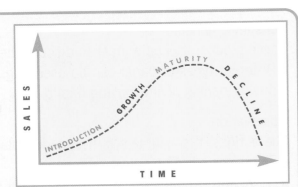

The product life-cycle

The various parts of a product's life form the **product life-cycle**.

- After being developed, the product is introduced on to the market.
- This **Introduction stage** is **associated with high advertising and other costs**, with the product making a loss because of this.
- **More consumers start buying the product in the Growth stage**; it increases its market share, establishes brand loyalty and becomes profitable.
- The product has its **maximum sales and profits during the Maturity stage**; it reaches market saturation and/or faces increasing competition.
- **It goes into Decline**, with falling sales and market share.

> *Remember that the life-cycle shows successful products only: most fail at or before the Introduction stage.*

Extending product life

Because it is so difficult to create successful products, businesses often try to extend the life of existing products. These **extension strategies** include:

- **changing use** – e.g. selling ice-cream forms of popular chocolate bars
- **changing packaging** – e.g. using it to emphasise a 'new improved model' approach.

Links

Broad links can be made between the product life-cycle and the 'Boston Box'.

LIFE-CYCLE

Introduction	⟷	Problem Child
Growth	⟷	Star
Maturity	⟷	Cash Cow
Decline	⟷	Dog

BOSTON BOX

Branding

By **branding** its product, the business guarantees to the onsumer that the next one bought will be virtually the same as the last one.

- This encourages repeat purchases through **brand loyalty**.

- Branding also helps the business differentiate – make different – its products from those of its competitors.

- **Mass advertising** becomes possible with branding.

KEY TERMS

Make sure you understand these terms before moving on!

- product mix
- Boston Matrix
- product life-cycle
- extension strategies
- branding
- brand loyalty
- mass advertising

QUICK TEST

1. Group the stages below under their correct headings:

Boston Box   **Life cycle**

Maturity,
Cash Cow,
Growth,
Decline,
Dog,
Star,
Introduction,
Problem Child

2. Identify two strategies used to extend the life of a product.

3. What is the 'product mix'?

Price

Pricing strategies for new products

Businesses use different strategies to price their new products. Incorrect pricing strategies mean the business will not find customers and therefore will lose income.

Penetration pricing

- A low price is set in the hope of gaining a high market share.
- The business will gain economies of scale, which help it keep the price low.
- The low price set may stop competitors from entering this market.

£95

Skimming

- The business brings out a new, unique product, which is the early market leader.
- This enables it to set a high price because there is no competition.
- The price falls when competitors with similar products enter the market.

Pricing tactics

Psychological pricing – a price is set just below a significant whole number, e.g. £9.95 rather than £10.00.

Capturing pricing – when a business makes both the 'hardware' and 'software' elements of a product (e.g. Nintendo, Sony and Sega game products), it may sell the hardware at a low price so that it can 'capture' the long-term sales on its high-priced software items.

£995

Discrimination pricing – the business sets **different prices in different segments** (e.g. railway off-peak and young-person fares are much lower than full-priced fares for the same journey).

Special offer pricing – e.g. a 'two for the price of one' tactic is used to encourage into the store customers who are then likely to buy other items. Some products may be sold by stores as **loss leaders** or below their cost price, again to tempt shoppers to enter the store.

Demand-based pricing

The basic law of supply and demand is that **demand falls as price increases and demand increases as price falls**. Price is therefore a major influence on the level of demand for products. Other influences on a product's demand include:

- **the availability of substitutes** for the business's product – the more substitutes there are available, the more sensitive the product will be to changes in its price (consumers will switch to the substitutes)

- **the level of consumer income** – in general, demand for a product increases as income levels increase

- **changes in consumer tastes** – demand will change as tastes change

- **how sensitive customers are to price** – they balance the price against other aspects, e.g. the product's status, quality, design and performance

Cost-based pricing

Accountants can calculate the **full cost** of making a product. Many businesses take this full-cost figure, and then include a **mark-up** so that a profit will be made.

- If the business uses cost-based pricing only, it may find competitors' prices are lower.

- In such cases, it will not be able to compete successfully on price.

profit

distribution

admin

labour

raw materials

QUICK TEST

1. State the pricing tactic that describes the following:

   a) 'Buy one, get one free'

   b) 'For sale, £4990'

   c) 'Hair cutting and styling for senior citizens, half-price every Thursday'

2. List three influences on the demand for a product.

Place

Distributing products

Place is **that part of the marketing mix that deals with distributing a business's products.**
- The business must get its products in the right amounts to the right market and at the right time, using the right **channel of distribution**.

Distribution channels

① **Through wholesaler and retailer to consumer**
- This is the traditional route for consumer goods.
- Agents may be used rather than wholesalers, e.g. in overseas markets.

② **Through wholesaler to consumer**
- This channel is sometimes used in high-population areas to sell consumer durables and other expensive items.

③ **Through retailer to consumer**
- Producers sell directly to the large-scale retailers that have their own large warehouses and who carry out their own wholesale function.
- Some producers set up (e.g. by franchising) their own retail outlets and sell their products using this distribution method.

④ **Direct to consumer**
- This direct selling route is often used by producers of industrial goods.
- It is popular in consumer goods markets (e.g. factory outlets, mail-order catalogues, leaflets through the post).

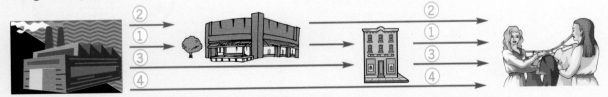

Selecting the channel

Selecting the distribution channel is influenced by:
- **the scale of the business** – large-scale businesses usually do their own distribution, e.g. owning their own transport fleet
- **the type of market** – e.g. a manufacturer selling goods nationally usually needs the support of both wholesalers and retailers
- **the product** – e.g. specialist goods with a limited demand often use direct channels
- the need to **balance the channel's cost against its efficiency** in getting the product to the consumer.

Wholesalers

Wholesalers are not as commonly used as they once were.
- Major retailers such as Tesco and Sainsbury have their own warehousing and distribution systems.
- The fall in the number of small-scale retailers has also affected wholesalers.

Traditional wholesalers still offer valuable services to both producers and retailers.

Services to the producer:
- **buying and storing in bulk** – this cuts the producer's distribution costs
- **advice and promotion** – feedback on the product's popularity can be given, and the wholesaler may help promote the product
- **taking on risk** – the wholesaler bears the risk of not selling the products.

Services to the retailer:
- **breaking bulk** – the wholesaler 'buys big' and 'sells small', cutting the retailer's storage costs
- **information and choice** – product information may be given
- **delivery and credit** – many wholesalers offer a delivery service for the smaller retailer, and their credit facilities help retailers finance their purchases.

E-commerce

Electronic commerce (**e-commerce**) is a popular development, now used by many businesses to sell their products.

Advantages to the business of using e-commerce include:
- **consumers can buy products 24 hours a day, seven days a week**
- it can be inexpensive to set up and operate
- since the Internet is international, the business can sell in new markets.

Problems of e-commerce include:
- many consumers lack the technology or expertise
- a lack of trust in buying over the Internet
- customers may simply be unaware of the e-commerce site.

KEY TERMS

Make sure you understand these terms before moving on!
- place
- channel of distribution
- wholesalers
- e-commerce

QUICK TEST

1. Tick the correct column:

	Service to producer	Service to retailer
a) Breaking bulk	☐	☐
b) Buying in bulk	☐	☐
c) Taking on risk	☐	☐
d) Offering credit	☐	☐

2. Products are needed in the right m_____ in the right a_____ at the right t_____. To do this, the right c_____ must be selected and used.

Promoting by advertising

Why businesses advertise

A business pays for **advertising** to:
- compete – to counter the advertising of competitors
- increase its sales – e.g. in a new market segment
- launch new products – customers need to find out about these
- improve its image – this 'corporate' or 'institution' advertising promotes the business name.

For and against advertising

Advertising:
- **informs** customers who otherwise may not find out about the product
- increases sales, which increases production and may bring about economies of scale
- encourages **competition**, which keeps prices down
- supports other industries (e.g. many newspapers survive through advertising revenue).

Advertising can be criticised for **exploiting** people by tempting them to buy:
- things they do not need
- what they cannot afford
- items that may do them harm (e.g. tobacco).

Persuasive and informative advertising

Persuasive advertising
- This seeks to make customers believe they need the business's product.
- It tempts consumers to buy the business's brand rather than competitor brands.

Informative advertising
- This form of advertising sets out to give customers information.
- It is often carried out by government and public bodies (public service advertising).

 In practice, many adverts are part persuasive and part informative.

Broadcasting media

These mass-market media are very popular, but can be very costly.

- TV advertising offers colour, sound and movement. It is the most expensive form of advertising, and only the larger companies tend to advertise on national television.
- Commercial radio is less costly, but lacks visual impact and has a smaller audience.
- The cinema can be used to target groups (e.g. the audience often has a high proportion of young people).

Print-based media

The business must choose from national (daily and Sunday papers), local (local papers) and specialist media (special-interest magazines).

- The advert is in a permanent form, and can be cut out and kept.
- It can also be linked with other promotion forms, e.g. competitions (sales promotion).
- These adverts often give more information than adverts in other media.
- Advertising in special-interest magazines means a business can sell to a specialist market.
- The advert tends to lack impact compared with broadcast media, since there is no sound and/or movement.

Outdoor media

- Posters are a popular form of outdoor advertising, attracting a large audience (e.g. placed by busy roads).
- Illuminated signs are widely used in city centres, attracting a large audience for little cost.

KEY TERMS

Make sure you understand these terms before moving on!
- advertising
- inform
- competition
- exploit
- persuasive advertising
- informative advertising

QUICK TEST

1. Advertising is p_____ for by a s_____ , and uses m_____ m_____ directed at a m_____ a_____.

2. List three reasons why a business chooses to advertise

3. Suggest a suitable advertising medium for the following:

   a) a local carnival is to take place

   b) a new washing powder is to be launched

   c) a political party wants to attack another party at a general election.

Other types of promotion

Sales promotion

These methods are used when marketers decide to promote their products by **directly encouraging people to buy them**. This is often achieved by offering incentives to buy. Branding and packaging are other important influences in sales promotion campaigns.

Types of sales promotion

Point-of-sale (POS) display

- Also known as merchandising, **this method promotes the product where it is sold**.
- Examples include using 'dump bins' by the till to sell sweets, encouraging impulse buying.

Promotion incentives

- Promotion incentives **tempt the consumer to buy particular brands**.
- They are commonly used by supermarkets and by producers whose goods are sold in them.
- Examples include multi-pack and money-off offers, price reductions, free gifts, competitions, and 'proof of purchase' refunds.

Other types

- **Exhibitions** are used to promote both consumer and industrial goods.
- **Sponsorship** and 'corporate entertainment' are often linked with major sporting events, and are used by larger businesses to promote their image.
- Offers of **after-sales service** and **guarantees** are used to encourage consumers to buy particular brands of products.

 The term 'below-the-line' promotion summarises these methods.

Direct marketing

Direct marketing methods are often used for niche market products. These methods involve **direct approaches to the customer**, and include:

- the use of mail order catalogues
- 'personal' letters and other direct mail ('junk mail')

Personal selling

This involves **face-to-face contact between the salesperson and the customer**. Although this is a labour-intensive and costly method, it offers several benefits:
- the salesperson can adjust the sales 'pitch' or offer promotional materials to persuade the customer to buy
- the customer can ask questions and the salesperson can give a demonstration or provide technical information if necessary.

Public relations

Although this is not a true form of promotion, public relations (PR) is often linked with it. Unlike advertising, **publicity** is not paid for by the business. The purpose of PR is to improve relations between a business and the public. To do this it:
- issues press releases to publicise good points about the business
- supports any 'corporate' advertising the business carries out.

AIDA

The **AIDA** approach is often used in promotion campaigns, especially for expensive items:
- the campaign attempts to capture the **attention** of would-be purchasers
- it tries to **interest** them in buying the product
- it creates a **desire** to own it
- this should lead to the **action** of buying the product.

KEY TERMS

Make sure you understand these terms before moving on!
- point-of-sale display
- promotion incentive
- exhibition
- sponsorship
- after-sales service
- guarantee
- direct marketing
- publicity
- AIDA

QUICK TEST

1. Tick the relevant column:

	Sales promotion	Personal selling	Direct marketing	Public relations
a) Junk mail	☐	☐	☐	☐
b) Visit by a salesman	☐	☐	☐	☐
c) Issuing a press release	☐	☐	☐	☐
d) Buy one get one free	☐	☐	☐	☐

2. Name four different methods of sales promotion.

Practice questions

Use the questions to test your progress.
Check your answers on page 95.

1. Analysing the market in order to identify different types of consumers is known as market _____ , and finding out their preferences is called market _____ .

2. One of the four Ps in the marketing mix is:
   a) profit ☐
   b) product ☐
   c) pollution ☐
   d) piece rate ☐

3. Which of these are examples of secondary (desk) research?
   a) looking at the firm's sales statistics ☐
   b) observing people doing their shopping ☐
   c) carrying out opinion polls ☐
   d) surveying people by telephone ☐
   e) reading government-produced statistics ☐

4. Which of the following are the responsibility of the marketing department?
   a) Interviewing job applicants ☐
   b) Buying new machinery ☐
   c) Undertaking market research ☐
   d) Planning how products are to be distributed ☐
   e) Carrying out sales promotion ☐
   f) Inspecting newly made products ☐
   g) Buying raw materials ☐
   h) Selling surplus equipment ☐

5. Name one suitable advertising medium for each of the following:
   a) a new GCSE Business Studies textbook ....
   b) a used Playstation ....
   c) a new mobile phone. ....

6. The PrettyPong range of cleaning products is made by Worth Ltd. The directors wish to introduce a 'new, environmentally-friendly PrettyPong' kitchen worktop and sink cleaning product. They hope to establish quickly a large market share in this highly competitive market.
   The Marketing Director of Worth Ltd has been asked to suggest whether the company should use skimming or penetration pricing for the new product, and how it should be promoted.
   a) Outline why branding is important to Worth Ltd.
   ....

   b) i) Explain the terms 'skimming' and 'penetration'.
   ....
   ....

   ii) Suggest which of these two strategies should be used for the new product. Give reasons for your answer.
   ....
   ....

   c) Explain how the directors will need to consider advertising when marketing the new product.
   ....

   d) Select **two** sales promotion methods the directors might use for the new product. Justify your choice.
   ....
   ....

7. Store-it Ltd manufactures and sells desks and storage units for home computers. These are sold directly by the company, as well as in major 'out-of-town' computer stores. The chart below shows the product life cycle for its 'TidyUp' product range.

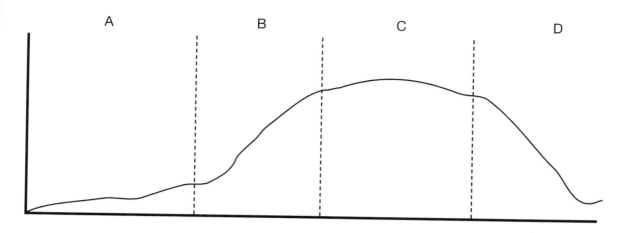

a) Suggest an appropriate title for the chart, and how the axes should be labelled.

....
....
....
....

b) i) Name each stage A, B, C and D.

....
....
....
....

ii) Describe what happens at each stage.

....
....
....
....

c) How might Store-it Ltd attempt to extend the life of its product ranges?

....
....
....

d) How might Store-it Ltd use market research to discover who is buying its products?

....
....
....
....

How well did you do?   ✗   1-2 **Start again**   3-4 **Getting there**   5-6 **Good work**   all 7 **Excellent!**   ✓

Answers

Our economy
Quick test answers

PAGE 5
1. Land, labour, capital, enterprise.
2. Demand for their products; influence of the government; social and environmental factors.
3. Advantage: employees are more efficient; disadvantage: employees may become bored with their work.

PAGE 7
1. a) Planned b) Free enterprise c) Free enterprise d) Planned

PAGE 9
1. d) primary; b) and e) secondary; a) and c) tertiary.
2. Cost; availability of labour; nature of the product; influence of the government.

PAGE 11
1. A charter protecting the rights of workers.
2. Eurozone: the member states who have signed up to the single currency. Euro: the name of the single currency.
3. Provide free movement of labour and goods, and establish common technical standards.

PAGE 13
1. Greater choice; lower prices through greater competition.
2. a) problems of different cultures and language; extra costs (e.g. transport) still have to be met; competition from EU-based and other firms; exchange rate difficulties.
   b) a single market with similar requirements for products (e.g. safety); paperwork and other administrative requirements are the same throughout the EU.

PAGE 15
1. Unlimited liability; separate legal existence.
2. a) one; b) there is no legal maximum.

PAGE 17
1. Private companies cannot sell their shares to the public; private company accounts are not available to the public.
2. Shareholders (owners) may wish the company to follow different policies from those the directors (controllers) want.
3. Incorporated businesses can take and defend legal actions in their own name; incorporated businesses have limited liability.

PAGE 19
1. Benefits: the multinational provides jobs, and brings in new ideas. Drawbacks: it is in a powerful position, and it can export its profits to its home country.
2. Franchisor; franchisees.
3. Retail; producer (worker).

PAGE 21
1. A person (or group of people) having a direct interest in an organisation's work and performance.
2. a) profit level; b) survival of the business; c) job security; d) quality of product; e) effect on the local environment; f) liquidity (can the business meet its debts?)

Pages 22–3 Answers to practice questions
1. House builder; car manufacturer; food-processing firm.
2. d) Labour.
3. The owners are limited to the amount they can lose in the business.
4. a) partnership; b) sole trader; c) partnership; d) public company; e) private company.
5. Price set by demand and supply. If demand exceeds supply, price rises, encouraging suppliers to make more and consumers to demand less. If supply exceeds demand, price falls, encouraging suppliers to make less and consumers to demand more. In both cases, eventually demand and supply reach 'equilibrium'.
6. a) Limited liability to protect the owners financially; separate legal existence, so the business can continue more easily if one of the owners leaves.
   b) The company's business affairs would remain more private; very costly to set up a PLC; owners risk losing direct control of the company.
7. a) i) Franchisee; ii) Franchisor.
   b) Advantages of receiving specialist support from franchisor, and being able to sell a range of recognised products; disadvantages of losing some control over business matters, and having to pay some profits to the franchisor.
   c) Survival; make an adequate profit.
   d) The petrol company will probably have objectives based on market share and keeping its shareholders contented.
8. a) Secondary sector, private sector.
   b) i) Shareholders, local community.
   ii) Shareholders are interested in the company's profitability and the security of their investment; local community in environmental matters and how the company supports their community (e.g. employment).
   c) Benefits: wider market (more sales and profits), diversifying into different markets (safer). Problems: setting up how to sell (getting information, channels of distribution), different language/culture (marketing problems), risk of failing to sell products in new markets (financial problems), having to face local competition, dealing in other currencies (UK not in Single Currency zone).
   d) Single market in EU (standard paperwork, no tariffs, easier procedures).
   e) Cost of land – more expensive in south-east England. Location to market – closer to rest of Europe, but may be further away from UK-based customers. Effect on employees – can/will they move with the company? Financing the move – how will the money be found?

Inside and Outside the Business
Quick test answers

PAGE 25
1. To make sure they have enough cash in the future.
2. The job description gives details of the job, person specification gives details of the person.
3. Advertising, sales promotion, direct marketing, personal selling.

PAGE 27
1. Span of control is the number of staff under a manager/supervisor; chain of command is how the hierarchy is organised.
2. To improve communication and decision-making, and to reduce the feeling of 'distance' between those at the top and those at the bottom of the hierarchy.

PAGE 29
1. Internal: managers, employees. External: shareholders, customers, suppliers, lenders, government.
2. Degree of formality required; whether permanent communication record is needed; volume of information; speed necessary; nature of information (e.g. whether technical or not).
3. Length of message; over-complex language used; 'noise'; missing out key information.

PAGE 31
1. a) Internal: growth within the organisation. External: growth that also involves another organisation.
   b) Mergers, by agreement; takeovers, when one company obtains full control of another.
   c) Horizontal: at same stage of production. Vertical: at different stage of production. Lateral: firms in different industries.
2. Economies of scale; greater chance of survival.
3. Profits; turnover; number of employees; capital employed.
4. Sell more products; sell new products; sell in a new market.

PAGE 33
1. Financial; information; exporting.
2. To remain competitive internationally; to encourage employment.
3. Regional Trends; Social Trends.

PAGE 35
1. Employment, discrimination, health and safety.
2. Lack of competition can lead to higher prices and exploitation of consumers.

PAGE 37
1. a) changing tastes; b) new production methods; c) change in interest rates; d) new consumer protection law.
2. Through improving the pay and working conditions of their members.
3. An organised group of people who share similar interests, and who wish to further their interests by influencing others.

Pages 38–9 Answers to practice questions
1. d) organisation chart.
2. c) laws.
3. a) advantage; b) advantage or disadvantage; c) disadvantage; d) advantage; e) disadvantage
4. Horizontal a) and e); vertical forwards b); vertical backwards d); lateral c).
5. i) b; ii) f; iii) e; iv) a; v) c; vi) e; vii) d.
6. Greater control over outlets, and therefore marketing and pricing policy. Greater control over supply, therefore more secure position. All profits made at all stages belong to the business.
7. a) Purchasing, technical support, maintenance.
   b) To deal with existing and potential staff; to recruit new staff (recruitment manager); to support existing staff (staff welfare manager); to train, negotiate with and administer staff (managers plus office staff).
   c) hierarchy: formal structure shown by the various levels in the chart; span of control: number of people under the control of one person, e.g. Production Controller's span includes Production Office staff; chain of command: control through the hierarchy, e.g. Financial Director to Accounts Office Manager, to Accounts Office staff.
   d) Clarifies the formal hierarchy and decision-making process; acts as a record; can use when inducting new staff to explain structure.
   e) i) Paying wages/salaries to new starters.
   ii) Memo: stating details of new starter and pay rate; email: to confirm payment made.
   iii) Reduces misunderstanding inside and outside the company; allows ideas and information to be transmitted efficiently; the more efficient communication is, the more profitable the company is likely to be.

People in Business
Quick test answers

PAGE 41
1. a) internal; b) external; c) external; d) internal.
2. a) 'job description'; b) 'person specification'.

PAGE 43
1. a) internal; b) external; c) internal
2. interviewed, training needs, targets.
3. Resources available (e.g. training staff); cost of the training.

PAGE 45
1. a) McGregor; b) Herzberg; c) Maslow; d) Maslow; e) Herzberg.
2. a) motivator; b) hygiene factor.

PAGE 47
1. Period of pay (week or month); location/nature of work (e.g. factory and office); amount is variable (wage) or fixed (salary).
2. Performance-related pay is based on the number of (satisfactory) items made; flat-rate systems ignore this.
3. a) Encourages staff loyalty and hard work b) staff feel directly involved in the success of the firm.

PAGE 49
1. Improve pay, improve conditions, protect members, provide services for members.
2. To support their member organisations; to persuade the government to adopt the policies they support.

PAGE 51
1. Employers and employees (e.g. through their union) negotiate pay and conditions.
2. Overtime ban, work-to-rule, go-slow, picketing, sit-in, strike.
3. Conciliation, arbitration, advice.

Pages 52–3 Answers to practice questions
1. Recruiting staff; keeping staff records; organising staff training.
2. c) a short list.
3. c) job description.

4. a) self-actualisation (or ego);
(b) social; (c) basic; (d) safety.
5. Decide what the training priorities are; analyse the jobs for which training is to be given; prepare training requirements; select the people to be trained.
6. a) i) New ideas introduced.
ii) Pay rates (competitive?); job prospects (promotion?); working conditions (pleasant?); number of people who can meet demands of the job (qualifications/skills?).
b) i) Overview of company history; tour of premises; meeting with staff from the department.
ii) New member feels motivated; makes an early contribution to the work.
c) External certificate/qualification likely; gaining wider knowledge and skills.
7. a) Identify feelings and wishes of members; negotiate with management to meet members' wishes.
b) Improving working conditions: e.g. hours of work, holidays, physical conditions.
c) Work-to-rule: employees follow the rule book precisely, which normally slows up production. Overtime ban: refuse to work above contracted hours, which may affect production and meeting any urgent orders.
d) Conciliation – meeting both parties to find 'common ground' to resolve dispute; arbitration – independent third party makes decision; on dispute information/advice – expertise offered.
8. a) Asks for young 'man', not 'person'.
b) Hours; location of work; contact address/phone number.
c) i) Time rate (overtime mentioned).
ii) Annual salary with or without commission/bonus on sales made.

Finance in Business
Quick test answers
PAGE 55
1. To start; to survive; to expand.
2. Shareholder – owns the company, receives dividend payments; debenture holder – lender to the company, receives interest payments.
3. a) trade credit; b) bank loan; c) share capital.
PAGE 57
a) v; b) iii; c)i; d) iv; e) ii.
PAGE 59
1. Profit states how much the business has earned; profitability measures this profit against the resources (capital employed) used in making it.
2. Current ratio; Quick Assets ratio.
PAGE 61
1. a) direct, variable; b) indirect, fixed; c) direct, (probably) fixed; d) indirect, fixed.
2. overheads, apportioned.
3. To compare actual costs with what was expected, and to study any differences (variances).
PAGE 63
1. Total costs, total revenue.
2. a) Break-even = £35 000/(£15 – £8) = 5 000 units; revenue = 5 000 x £15 = £75 000.
b) Margin of safety = (8 000 – 5 000) 3 000 units.
PAGE 65
1. Controls expenditure; motivates managers; forces people to plan ahead.
2. Source of cash b), c) and d); Use of cash a) and e).

Pages 66–7 Answers to practice questions
1. Calculating financial ratios; preparing financial statements.
2. d) Output.
3. c) Production figures.
4. b) Creditors.
5. A profit and loss account; a cash flow statement.
6. Cost of borrowing: how much, and for how long?; length of time the finance is needed for: short-term, medium-term or long-term?
7. a) £51 000/200 = £255 each.
b) £52 000 – £51 000 = £1000 (£50 each).
c) Fixed cost element is included in the average cost calculation and not the variable cost calculation.
8. a) Profitability: return on capital employed (ROCE) 30/1500 = 2%; gross profit margin 150/600 = 25%, net profit margin 30/600 = 5% liquidity: current ratio 150 to 100 = 1.5 to 1; quick assets 100 to 100 = 1 to 1.
b) Profitability, 2p net profit from every £1 capital used to make this profit (very low return); 25p in the £ gross profit and 75p in the £ cost of sales; 5p in the £ net profit, liquidity, sufficient current assets, even excluding stock, to meet current liabilities.
c) Previous results, and/or competitors' results.
9. a) Contribution £3 – £1 (80p+20p) = £2
Break-even = fixed costs £8000 divided by £2 = 4000 T-shirts.
b) Break-even chart
i) Break-even 4000; ii) break-even revenue £12 000 (proof: 4000 x £3); iii) profit £4000 (£18 000 – £14 000); iv) margin of safety 2000 units (6000 – 4000).

Making the Products
Quick test answers
PAGE 69
1. a) mass; b) job; c) batch; d) mass; e) job.
2. Advantage: efficient use of labour and equipment. Disadvantage: employees become bored.
PAGE 71
1. a) financial; b) purchasing; c) managerial; d) risk-bearing.
2. Internal are within the firm; external exist within the whole industry.
PAGE 73
1. Output, inputs, per employee, competitive, unit costs, fall.
2. CAD is concerned with the design, and CAM with the manufacture, of products.
PAGE 75
1. storage, out of date, out of stock, custom(ers).
2. a) a quality system that seeks to get things 'right first time'; b) a system used to minimise stock costs; c) the most economic quantity to reorder.

Pages 76–7 Answers to practice questions
1. b) Bridges.
2. Undertaking quality control, measuring productivity.
3. a) iii; b) iv; c) vi; d) i; e) ii; f) v.
4. a) 1) f) iii; 2) h) iv; 3) b) i; 4) d) viii; 5) c) v; 6) g) ii; 7) a) vi; 8) e) vii.
b) Concentration, Reputation, Information.
5. a) i) job, ii) batch.
b) Greater chance of economies of scale (e.g. bulk buying); labour may be less skilled (less expensive); more machines may be used (quicker production).
6. a) The unit cost price falls as output increases.
b) Purchasing economies: likely,

e.g. due to bulk buying of components for the screens; technical economies: likely due to specialist manufacturing equipment needed for computer screens.
c) After 8000, diseconomies of scale seem to start (unit cost rises to £41). 8000 also gives maximum profit: £12 (selling less cost) x 8000 = £96 000, largest figure obtainable (next largest = £13 x 7000 = £91 000).
7. a) i) Batch: set number of products made, before production switches to another model, e.g. baking batches of different loaves of bread; mass: one production line devoted exclusively to making a single product, e.g. mass-produced chocolate bars.
ii) Either could be suitable, depending on demand. Mass production if sweeteners sold nationally in bulk; batch production to meet particular orders from sweet/chocolate manufacturers.
b) i) 'Get it right first time/more right next time' approach, where everyone is involved in continual improvement to his/her work.
ii) Foodstuff production demands highest quality, so TQM appropriate.
Employee involvement through, e.g. quality circles.

Selling the Products
Quick test answers
PAGE 79
1. Age; sex; income/social class; lifestyle.
2. Product, price, distribution (place), promotion.
3. (e.g. McDonald's) strength, known brand; weakness, coping with orders at peak times; opportunity, expansion through franchising; threat, increasing demand for vegetarian foods.
PAGE 81
1. Face-to-face interviews, telephone surveys, postal surveys.
2. Local chambers of commerce, banks, the CBI.
PAGE 83
1. Boston Box: Cash Cow, Dog, Star, Problem Child; Life-cycle: Introduction, Growth, Maturity, Decline.
2. Changes in use; changes in packaging.
3. The range of products marketed by the business.
PAGE 85
1. a) Special offer pricing; b) psychological pricing; c) discrimination pricing.
2. Consumer income levels, consumer tastes, consumer sensitivity to price.
PAGE 87
1. a) retailer; b) producer; c) producer; d) retailer.
2. Market, amount, time, channel.
PAGE 89
1. paid, sponsor, mass media, mass audience.
2. Compete with others, inform customers of new products, increase market share.
3. a) local radio/local paper/leaflet in paper or through door; b) national TV; c) roadside poster.
PAGE 91
1. a) direct marketing; b) personal selling; c) PR; d) sales promotion.
2. POS display, promotion incentives, exhibitions, sponsorship.

Pages 92–3 Answers to practice questions
1. Segmentation, research.

2. b) Product.
3. a) and e).
4. Undertaking market research; carrying out sales promotion.
5. a) Leaflets from the publisher distributed to schools.
b) Advert in a local paper.
c) TV adverts.
6. a) Enables Worth Ltd to advertise and market the product; leads to repeat purchases from consumers; establishes brand loyalty.
b) i) Skimming: sets high market price; penetration: sets low price.
ii) Penetration: the market is already established, so the company is not first into the market and cannot be a price leader; a competitive market exists, and the company wants a high share of this; a low-price policy is therefore needed to encourage many consumers to buy.
c) The directors need to do the following: identify which segments the company will focus on for marketing and advertising; select appropriate media from those available to the company; decide the extent to which the advertising will inform consumers, or persuade people to buy; establish an overall advertising strategy (e.g. which advertising agency to use); discuss how advertising is to be supported by other promotion methods.
d) Free samples: allows consumers to try product, the sample could be supported by 'money off' coupon for first purchase or for another 'PrettyPong' product. Premium offers: e.g. consumer collects labels from first two purchases, sends label to company and receives another 'PrettyPong' product free. Both strategies encourage repeat purchases and/or promote other products in the range.
7. a) Title: Store-it Ltd. Product life cycle, TidyUp range. Vertical axis: Sales (£ or units). Horizontal axis: Time.
b) i) A introduction, B growth, C maturity, D decline.
ii) Introduction, product launched on market with low sales and high promotion and other expenditure; not established, and risk of failure. Growth, product being bought in greater numbers though still heavily promoted; repeat purchases and brand loyalty becoming established. Maturity, product at peak of sales; large market share and profits, but market gradually becoming saturated. Decline, sales and profits fall as other products become more competitive or interesting to consumers; heavy promotion, or attempt to extend life through various offers.
c) Modifying the product in some way (e.g. new design, new colours); reducing price; selling in new market or new segment (e.g. as commercial office equipment).
d) Primary (field) research: e.g. questionnaires, for customers at the computer stores or those buying directly from the company. Secondary (desk) research: e.g. studying statistics on computer sales, checking own sales data.

Index